Herbert Marcuse's Utopia

Deposited in the Bibliothèque Nationale of Quebec,
3rd Quarter 1986
Typography and Cover: Naoto Kondo

Printed in Canada
First Harvest House Edition

For information address:
Harvest House Ltd.,
Suite 1, 1200 Atwater Ave.,
Montreal, Canada H3Z 1X4

Canadian Cataloguing in Publication Data

Martineau, Alain
Herbert Marcuse's utopia

Includes index.
Bibliography: p.
ISBN 0-88772-027-7

1. Marcuse, Herbert, 1898- 2. Philosophers—United States—Biography. 3. Utopias.
I. Title.

B945.M.2984M37 1986 191 C86-090243-9

Herbert Marcuse's Utopia

by
Alain Martineau

Translated by
Jane Brierley

Harvest House
MONTREAL 1986

To the memory of my father
and to my mother
without whom my education
would have been impossible

Translator's Note

I would like to thank the author, Dr. Alain Martineau, for his generous cooperation, despite a busy teaching and research schedule, in discussing the text and providing material for many of the English citations throughout the work. In the course of translation, the author has taken the opportunity to make slight changes or clarifications to the original manuscript for the benefit of English-speaking readers. My thanks are also due to Drew McCarthy, for reading the manuscript and notes.

Not all of Marcuse's translated writing is the same as the original, for he too sometimes took the opportunity of adding, retouching, or even revising his work for publication in another language. Texts that were originally speeches, or recorded question-and-answer periods, do not always contain identical material in English and French versions. Wherever possible, the published English version has been quoted. Where this proved impossible or impracticable, the translator has provided an English rendition, but the citation refers to the original work. The same method has been used for other writers cited in this book.

Contents

Acknowledgments

This translation, as well as the original work, has been published with the help of a grant from the Canadian Federation for the Humanities, using funds provided by the Social Sciences and Humanities Research Council of Canada. We also gratefully acknowledge a translation grant from the Canada Council.

Introduction

We only seem to have absorbed what we don't understand about Marcuse.[1]

There are many utopias. No one has ever seen them except in imagination, and yet they are real enough, for they have influenced our destiny over the centuries. Utopias are created in response to the existing world. Just as the worlds of Plato, Sir Thomas More, and Karl Marx differed, so did their philosophical utopias. It is Herbert Marcuse's utopia that has made him so significant and controversial a figure in our generation, and possibly for generations to come.

Marcuse endeavored to describe a viable alternative to the present dilemma of civilization through the projection of utopian ideals, and to liberate humans from the repressive forces of modern society in order to build a better world. Not surprisingly, his philosophical ideas took shape in relation to socialist and Marxist theory and its application to reality. Unlike many of his utopian predecessors, including Marx, he was privileged to witness the progress of a full-scale social experiment based on a philosophical concept.

Marx wrote in his 1844 "Contribution to the Critique of Hegel's Philosophy of Law" that the *head* of man's "emancipation is *philosophy*, its *heart* is the *proletariat*. Philosophy cannot be made a reality without the abolition of the proletariat, the proletariat cannot be abolished without philosophy being made a reality."[2] Marx's programmatic statement did not mean that philosophy is doomed, however. As Henri Lefebvre remarked in 1947, "It is not a question of *suppressing* philosophy, but of *making it a reality* by transcending abstract philosophy and by suppressing the abstract element of speculative, metaphysical philosophy."[3] Gérard Raulet, in a fairly recent study of Marxism and critical theory, noted that Marcuse's aim in 1937 was to give philosophy status within Marxism, as demonstrated in the following passage from "Philosophy and Critical Theory": "Bourgeois society's domination reveals itself not only in the dependence of thought but also in the (abstract) independence of its contents. For this society determines consciousness such that the latter's activity and contents survive in the dimension of abstract reason; abstractness saves its truth. What is true is so only to the extent that it is not the truth about social reality. And just because it is not the latter, because it transcends this reality, it can become a matter for critical theory."[4]

Dialectical materialism therefore has idealistic components that will be necessary, said Marcuse, "as long as the reality toward which they are directed is not yet given."[5] But how can or must philosophy be made reality? If, according to Marx's eleventh thesis on Feuerbach, "The philosophers have only *interpreted* the world in various ways; the point is to *change* it,"[6] then philosophy ought to play an active part in its own realization. Far from being a sign of realization, however, the current fragmentation of philosophy into various subdisciplines seems more like a symptom of disintegration. Will there be a complete break between past and future philosophy? How are we to consider the problem of modernity in philosophy today? One thing is certain: such questions must be examined in relation to Marxist theory.

Prior to Marx, the accepted model of philosophical debate was the famous *querelle des Anciens et des Modernes* in the French Academy, embodying a confrontation between two camps. One camp advocated exploiting the past in order to prolong it, while the other placed greater reliance on the future and sought to promote new theories. The question is, has one of these camps now gained ascendancy? With Marx himself, we are still looking at a model with dual tendencies. In his most traditional stance, Marx retained his belief in progress and the importance of Reason. He declined to formulate a philosophical program as such, however, and instead constituted himself the theoretician of social practice. But do we still take into consideration these two aspects of Marx's thought? Post-Marxian discourse takes it for granted that the philosophical process occurs within the current social context. Yet philosophers, even Marxist philosophers, try to maintain a certain detachment from this context, the better to fully comprehend it. We can therefore say that there are still two tendencies influencing the debate on modernity.

At present, however, we are being forced to consider the fundamental nature of modernity in a new light. The distinctive feature of our time seems to be a state of general and permanent crisis, a crisis that is unique in history and conditioned by an unprecedented technological explosion. In days gone by, during the Renaissance for example, humanism encouraged man's self-awareness in order to combat the mysticism of the medieval world. Today, in a world "disenchanted" by science and technology, mysticism is being rediscovered in numerous and varied forms. Sixteenth-century moderns relied on the future to change society. The Marxist revolutionary spirit counted on class war to bring about abrupt historical change and alter social structures. Present-day proponents of this revolutionary spirit, disillusioned by the practices and regimes invoked in the name of Marxism, are burning their idols and looking toward a movement or a revolution with no predetermined model. Yet, when we look at the so-called cultural revolution and the phenomena of consciousness-raising, counterculture, protest, or even libertarian socialism, certain common features become apparent. In a word, there is a renewed sense of modernity in our contemporary society.

One of the major aspects of this modernist current seems to me to be *The Spirit of Utopia*, to use Ernst Bloch's expression. The present interest in utopia is no coincidence. Intoxicated by the frenetic pace of technology, and deprived of the traditional heritage of communal knowledge, contemporary man thinks he can see what Marcuse calls "the end of utopia"—the possibility of realizing the wildest dreams of the utopians. Classical utopia as a literary genre is dead, although in a sense it survives in the form of dystopia. Utopianism has endured, however, despite this eclipse. It defined the mental atmosphere of the New Left, of which, rightly or wrongly, Marcuse was considered a guru. As a Marxist philosopher and sociologist, Marcuse was consciously utopian,[7] as well as being concerned with "the most . . . 'eschatological' conceptions of Marxian theory."[8] It is important that we understand Marcuse's contribution to contemporary utopianism. Our present situation may indeed be such that we desperately need utopianism to buttress critical and philosophical thought.

Marcuse thought so. He devoted his life's work to finding an alternative to the status quo, which is essentially distinguished by the absence of one particular event: the revolution that has not yet happened, that *cannot* happen under present historical conditions, but that, as a preparatory measure, he attempted to justify in advance, so as to halt the growing and excessive repression of natural aspirations for happiness and freedom. Marcuse's sole project was to redefine "socialism and its preconditions,"[9] and to take a fresh view of "the conception of the transition to socialism."[10] In so doing, he used "the concept of a non-repressive way of life to demonstrate that a new stage of civilization is now possible."[11] All the material and intellectual preconditions for a socialist society exist. The only thing standing in its way is the repressive organization of the existing forces of production.[12] For Marcuse, therefore, the transition from capitalism to socialism cannot be defined as the planned development of the means of production and the rationalization of resources, even though such rationalization is still a precondition of liberation in any form. It is only "if socialism is defined in its most utopian terms," that it can be "a force for transformation of human existence and of its environment."[13] Marcuse was only concerned with libertarian socialism—"a socialism that does not yet actually exist."[14] Contrary to Engels, Marcuse urged, "We must face the possibility that the path to socialism may proceed from science to utopia and not from utopia to science."[15] Bloch held a similar view. Just as Marx foresaw the realization of philosophy, so Marcuse foresaw the realization of utopia. As he himself said, "The utopian element was long the only progressive element in philosophy."[16] This is why utopian thought is necessary to philosophy in general, and to critical theory in particular.

In sum, does the contemporary utopianism underlying all Marcuse's work oblige us to redefine modernity? We must recognize the fact that Marx's collective aim has not been achieved, and that all past revolutions have ended in disillusionment. Nevertheless, we should also realize that the revolutionary spirit still inspires hope, especially when coupled with a utopian faith that includes the elements described by Leszek Kolakowski: the belief that we can control our future, the persistent idea that effective theory and action do in fact exist, and the conviction that we can understand the true nature of man.[17] It is these basic questions that I have endeavored to explore.

In dealing with Marcuse's utopia, I have begun by outlining its development, linking the various phases of his life to his principal theses. I have adopted a historical approach because, apart from Sidney Lipshires' work,[18] biographical information is fairly sparse. Recent monographs published since his death do not fill the gap. Neither Morton Schoolman[19] nor Vincent Geoghegan[20] provide an actual biography, although Barry Katz's relatively recent book, *Herbert Marcuse and the Art of Liberation*, gives considerable detail. I have to a great extent relied on commentary by the people who knew him, and their various accounts have proved very useful throughout this work. The area of Marcuse's relationships with his colleagues in the Frankfurt School has already been amply covered, however. Martin Jay has written a definitive history of the group.[21] David Held summarized its principle ideas brilliantly,[22] while George Friedman brought together its political philosophy.[23] Gérard Raulet demonstrated Marcuse's place in critical theory, in its wider or revised context.[24] The work of Ben Agger, notably his introduction to Western Marxism, has provided an extended synthesis of Marxism and American populism, somewhat in the style of Marcuse.[25]

The second chapter documents the background of Marcusian utopianism, tracing the connection between Marcuse and his major utopian predecessors in order to further our understanding of the role of utopia in critical theory and its subversive function in society. The subsequent chapters form a critique of Marcusian utopianism in relation to man's four basic activities: art, economics, politics, and ethics. I have adopted a Marcusian approach to the question asked by Marx in his 1858 introduction to *Capital*: What is it that gives art an eternal value despite its historical nature? In addition I have looked at the place assigned by Marcuse to politics, in relation to the Marxist view of economics. Finally, I have considered the place of ethics in Marcuse's scheme for liberation.

In general, I have attempted to examine the following question: Does the hope of modernity lie with Marcuse's utopia? Utopianism is "a perennial type of thinking as ineradicable as realistic philosophy itself," according to Thomas Molnar. It is a system of thought or philosophy that, far from representing an aberration of the modern mind, attacks the major problems of existence, just as the authentic philosophers do.[26] I refer to Molnar because he is considered "one of the rare reactionary writers worth reading," according to Jean-Marie Domenach in "Utopia or Reason in the Imaginary World," an introduction to a special issue of *Esprit*.[27] Although Marcuse's utopia has its roots in a tradition as old as thought itself, it represents a fresh initiative. It is an attempt to conceive of social change, not in the light of class conflict, but of a critical theory that is itself basic to the change in question. Marcuse's utopia, while Marxist in nature, is the very opposite of specialized theory, for the perspective that he embraced was universal.

Alain Martineau

I

Marcuse the Man

Herbert Marcuse was born of Jewish parents, Carl Marcuse and Gertrud Kreslawsky, on July 19, 1898, in Berlin—a birthplace that some socialists might have considered a misfortune. Marcuse, however, was always proud of his Berlin origins. He said it was probably because of the Berliners' sense of humour.[1]

On the subject of Marcuse and his Judaic heritage, his third wife, Erica Sherover, and his son, Peter, told the press at the time of his death: "Although he was not religious, it was important for him . . . that he was Jewish," particularly with respect to the idea of using "life to help bring about a better life."[2] As Gershom Scholem explained in his book of essays on contemporary Judaism, *Fidelité et utopie*, when one views present history as the prehistory of humanity, or links liberation and the self-determination of human beings to the effects of a redemptive critique, "All discussion of real and authentic human values is reduced to eschatology. It opens the way to an impenitent and optimistic utopia, which cannot be described in terms of concepts based on an unredeemed world. This is the attitude underlying the writings of the major ideologists of revolutionary messianism, such as Ernst Bloch, Walter Benjamin, Theodor Adorno, and Herbert Marcuse, whose ties with their Jewish heritage, whether acknowledged or not, are evident."[3] Such was the case with Marcuse in his commentary on Walter Benjamin's philosophy of history, when he said, "Peace (in Kant's sense of 'perpetual peace') represents the end of the prehistory of humanity, which has become history. True peace is real, materialist 'redemption,' non-violence, the advent of 'the just man' . . . therefore redemption is a materialist and political concept: the concept of Revolution."[4]

Obviously one's origins do not account for everything. I have therefore thought it worthwhile to outline the main stages of Marcuse's life as a background to his evolving thought. These stages fall quite naturally into the following periods:

- The Weimar period (1919-1933) of political involvement
- The Frankfurt School period (1934-1942) in the United States
- The Washington period (1942-1949) of literary silence
- The Brandeis period (1950-1965) of growing radicalization
- The San Diego period (1965-1979) of fame and notoriety
- The period of posterity (1979-)

Marcuse himself acknowledged in 1972 that the influence of the Weimar culture had marked him forever.[5] The Weimar Republic, as historians have labeled it, covered the fourteen years (1919-1933) of liberal democracy during which the Social Democrats played a dominant role either in government or opposition. The Social Democratic Party is one of the oldest major political parties in Germany. It originated with two groups—one Marxist, the other reformist—although it actually reflected several tendencies. But in 1918 Germany lost the war and social democracy was anything but revolutionary. It even opposed the Spartacist movement, which came into being in 1914 in response to the voting of funds for World War I. In 1916 this movement adopted the name *Spartakusbund*, after the slave revolt led by Spartacus against the Romans in 73 A.D. Its leading activists in 1918 were Karl Liebknecht (1871-1919) and Rosa Luxemburg (1871-1919), who advocated dictatorship of the proletariat and the formation of workers' councils on the Russian model.

Marcuse did his military service from 1917 to 1919. In 1917-1918 he was a member of the Social Democratic Soldiers' Council in Berlin, although his sympathy with the German Social Democratic party did not last long. Nevertheless, this brief period taught him the following lesson: "I resigned from it after the murder of Rosa Luxemburg and Karl Leibknecht, and from then on I have criticized this party's politics. Not because it believed that it could work within the framework of the established order—for we all do this, we all make use of even the most minute possibilities in order to transform the established order from inside it—that is not why I fought the S.P.D. The reason was rather that it worked in alliance with reactionary, destructive, and repressive forces."[6] Marcuse's subsequent thinking was influenced by this idea of political confrontation outside active politics, and indeed he admitted in 1978 that his political convictions were already firmly established at the time of the Weimar Republic, that he was *revolutionary*, and that *his philosophical inquiries gradually became part of his political beliefs.*[7] As the heir to the Luxemburgist left, wrote Jóhann Páll Arnason, Marcuse and the other Frankfurt theorists held "firmly to the principle that this revolution must be linked to the democratic and humanist ideals of the bourgeois period."[8] This is what Marcuse meant when he wrote, "It is by looking to the past, not the future, that the fight for freedom finds its strength."[9]

After the Luxemburg-Leibknecht murders, Marcuse's concrete political involvement was to remain extremely limited, although significant. It was limited in the sense that his sympathy for Marxism did not restrict his critical faculties. This was true of all the members of the Frankfurt School. They disapproved, for example, of the Moscow trials of 1936-1938 during the Stalin purges.[10] When Marcuse did make a political gesture, it was significant because his public involvement was not a response to his judgment of a particular event, but a defense of the individual. This was the case with his former student Angela Davis to whom he wrote an open letter in *Ramparts Magazine* at the time of her imprisonment.[11] Similarly, when Rudolf Bahro was imprisoned in East Germany, Marcuse made a point of producing a detailed study of *The Alternative*.[12] As for student protests, even though he hailed their potentially revolutionary tendencies, he later acknowledged that they had not produced the effect expected and were not sufficient to trigger true qualitative change.[13] Basically, his political views were often far more moderate than his critics may have thought. Douglas Kellner tells us that Marcuse supported Eugene McCarthy in 1968 and George McGovern in 1972.[14]

All in all, his commitment was that of an intellectual more interested in cultural values than civilization, and in this he reflected the German Weimar period.[15] In l914, the French set out to defend civilization, whereas the Germans asserted that they were fighting for their culture.[16] Marcuse, in the tradition of German idealism, had such abnormally high expectations for humanity that, as his *Time* biographer said, he "came to the conclusion that only revolution could realize them."[17] After his participation in the Soldiers' Council, he never joined another political party.

In 1919 Marcuse began his studies at Freiburg University where, he said, life and politics did not mix.[18] It was here in 1922 that he received a doctorate *magna cum laude* for his dissertation, "Der deutsche Künstlerroman," on German novels dealing with the lives of artists. We will be looking at the role of art in Marcuse's revolution later, but I should point out now that in the Germany of 1919, several groups had formed that were interested in revolutionary art. Jean-Michel Palmier wrote about these groups in his contribution to *L'Expressionisme comme révolte*, a book on the artistic life of the Weimar Republic. He recognized that it is not easy, for example, to analyze the political ideas of the Novembergruppe, or to define art as a revolutionary weapon, since "utopian and realist elements were intertwined."[20]

During the six years that followed, between the ages of 25 and 31, Marcuse worked in publishing and bookselling in Berlin.[21] In 1929 he returned to Freiburg University. It was to some extent the political climate of the period that influenced his intellectual interests. He wrote, "It was evident that fascism was coming and that led me to an intensive study of Marx and Hegel . . . with the aim of understanding just why, at a time when the conditions for an authentic revolution were present, the revolution had collapsed or been defeated, the old forces had come back to power, and the whole business was beginning all over again in a degenerate form."[22] So there he was, a student at the age of 31 under Husserl and Heidegger, among others. The latter directed his major dissertation on Hegel, published in 1932. But the Marxist orientation evident in his early articles meant that he was moving away from Heidegger, who tended more toward the right. Since Marcuse could not become Heidegger's assistant and had no idea where to find work, Husserl asked Kurt Riezler of Frankfurt University to give him a recommendation. Riezler, an enthusiastic admirer of Heidegger,[23] approached Horkheimer, director of the university's Institute for Social Research. Its founders had not dared call it the Marxist Institute—such a name would have been too provocative[24]—and its work was formulated in Hegelian terms in order to disguise its Marxism. According to Marcuse, this precaution was justified by the desire "to maintain their foothold in the academic world."[25]

Marcuse's first article in 1928, "Contributions to a Phenomenology of Historical Materialism," revealed both his Marxist orientation and his interest in Heidegger's theories, since it was published in a special issue of *Philosophische Hefte* on *Being and Time*. During his four years at Freiburg, Marcuse prepared his doctoral dissertation on "Hegel's Ontology and the Theory of Historicity," as well as publishing nearly a dozen articles, six of which appeared in the German Social Democratic review, *Die Gesellschaft Internationale Revue für Sozialismus und Politik*. This period was characterized by a crucial debate: Marx or Heidegger? Superficially, Marcuse appeared to have decided in favor of Marx, for he was far more of a Marxist than an ontologist. In the deeper sense, however, he was indelibly marked by Heidegger. Just as for Heidegger, philosophy involved harking back to the Greeks, so for Marcuse, philosophy meant harking back, but from Marx to the latter's philosophical past.

The achievements of the Weimar period can be summed up as follows. In 1928, Marcuse provided the first example of phenomenological Marxism, viewing the young Marx from the standpoint of existential phenomenology. In 1932, he was the first in Germany to devote a major commentary to Marx's *Economic and Philosophical Manuscripts of 1844*, as well as being among the first to suggest a new interpretation of Marxism based on Marx's early writings.[26] This Heideggerian Marxism anticipated that of Jean-Paul Sartre, Karl Kosik, Enno Paci, and others. Moreover, it extended the Hegelian Marxism of Lukács and Korsch, centered on the theory of class consciousness that they had developed to explain why the working class failed in its revolt against capitalism. But these major Marxist preoccupations should not obscure Marcuse's critical distance from Marxism *per se*, as can be seen in his other studies of the same period on Karl Mannheim, Wilhelm Dilthey, and Hans Freyers.

During the 1930s Marcuse worked with the Frankfurt School, the group whose history has been so definitively set forth by Martin Jay.[27] When the Nazis took power on January 30, 1933, the Institute moved to Geneva. It was here that Marcuse, at the age of 35, began his teaching career. He taught sociology for ten years, although he did not confine himself to this one subject, since the avowed aim of the International Institute for Social Research, as it was now called, was the interdisciplinary study of problems encountered in social theory, for the purpose of arriving at a comprehensive theory of society.[28] When Marcuse joined the group it was composed of Max Horkheimer (philosopher, sociologist, and social psychologist), Friedrich Pollock (economist and specialist in problems of national planning), Leo Lowenthal (a student of literature and popular culture), Erich Fromm (psychoanalyst and social psychologist), Franz Neumann (political scientist specializing in law), and Theodor Adorno (philosopher, sociologist, and musicologist).[29]

In July 1934, Marcuse, accompanied by his first wife, Sophie, and his son, Peter, traveled to Columbia University in New York. There, as a lecturer in sociology, he continued to work with the other members of the Institute, for during the same year the Institute—revolutionary and Marxist though it was—also moved to new quarters in the heart of the world's largest capitalist city, at the same time becoming affiliated with Columbia University.[30] Despite the massive influx of German intellectuals to the United States at that time, this move was something of a surprise, since it ran counter to Marx's expressed views. When Cabet suggested that the French communists form a utopian community in "Icaria," by which was meant the free American states or California, Marx apparently opposed the scheme because he felt that the establishment of communal ownership presupposed its accomplishment in the here and now, not in another time or place.[31] Marcuse, in his preface to the original edition of *Reason and Revolution*, went so far as to flatter his American public by referring to Hegel's description of America as the only "land of the future."[32] In the context, however, it seems that the move was dictated by circumstances.

If ever there was a Frankfurt School, it was never in Frankfurt, but in New York in the 1930s, in the house on 117th Street lent by Columbia University. Marcuse described life at the Institute in answer to a query from Habermas.[33] Its main activity was to publish work in the official review of the Institut für Sozialforschung, the *Zeitschrift für Socialforschung*. The selection of articles was discussed in Horkheimer's office. Those who happened to be there could take part. For a variety of personal reasons, the group was divided into two camps: on one side, Otto Kirchheimer, a political scientist specializing in law like Neumann, and Henryk Grossman, a political economist; on the other, Pollock, Lowenthal, Adorno, Marcuse, and Horkheimer. Manuscripts were usually submitted to Lowenthal, then to

Horkheimer, after which they were discussed in seminars, either with Columbia students or the general public. Marcuse's contribution included seven articles and over fifty reviews covering about 150 books.

In 1937, Horkheimer published an article entitled "Traditional and Critical Theory" in *Zeitschrift für Socialforschung*.[34] He distinguished theory, in the traditional sense of Descartes' *Discourse on Method*, from the critical theory of society, which originated in Marx's critique of political economy.[35] A few months later he added an "Appendix,"[36] to which Marcuse responded in his article "Philosophy and Critical Theory."[37] Generally speaking, the expression "critical theory" denoted the theoretical position taken by the Frankfurt School, which sought to revise Marxist social theory while remaining, according to their way of thinking, faithful to the Marxist spirit.[38]

Interpretations of this position varied so widely, however, that the principal figures of the school, such as Horkheimer, Adorno, and Marcuse, gave it a very different theoretical and practical meaning. In 1970, William Leiss, interested in working with those who wanted to bring about genuinely human change and revitalize the intellectual foundations of the modern revolutionary tradition, underscored these differences when discussing how to implement an adequate theory of contemporary political action.[39] Whereas Marcuse had become publicly involved in the campaign against the war in Vietnam, for example, Horkheimer was fairly sympathetic to the United States. And while Marcuse was sympathetic to student protest, Adorno took a very different view.[40]

Marcuse contended that for him critical theory was essentially based on two premises, which he put forward at every opportunity,[41] and formulated in *One-Dimensional Man* as follows: "Any critical theory of society . . . implies value judgments: . . . the judgment that human life is worth living. . . . the judgment that, in a given society, specific possibilities exist for the amelioration of human life and specific ways and means of realizing these possibilities."[42]

This second Marcuse period was marked by two significant events. The first was his being chosen in 1937 to reply to Horkheimer's article on critical theory.[43] One might go so far as to say that he adopted the Frankfurt master's conclusion as a personal motto: "The future of humanity depends on the existence today of the critical attitude."[44] The second event was the 1941 publication of *Reason and Revolution*, with which he became the first to present "critical theory" and its ideas to an English-speaking public.[45]

After the publication of *Reason and Revolution* and a reply to a review by Karl Löwith, there began a long period of what can be termed literary silence, broken only by five reviews. However, one of these, on Sartre's *L'Etre et le Néant*, was more substantial than the rest.

Marcuse spent eight years of his life working for the American government, starting in 1942. Although, as Martin Jay remarked, "This was not precisely what the Frankfurt School had meant when it advocated revolutionary *praxis*,"[46] Marcuse explained that he tried "to do everything that was in [his] power to help defeat the Nazi regime."[47]

Between the ages of 44 and 52, therefore, Marcuse worked for two military intelligence services: first the Office of War Information, and then the O.S.S. or Office of Strategic Services, where he ended up as interim director of the Western European Section after working under his friend Franz Neumann.[48] He stayed on in Washington after the war to work in the first large-scale American espionage agency, because his wife developed cancer and they were unable to leave. He himself said that we "must abstract" this period.[49]

In 1950-195l, when he was 52, he gave a series of lectures at the Washington School of Psychiatry,[50] in which he suggested that psychological and political modes form a dialectical unit, and that if this unit can be penetrated it might be possible to "explode" the irrationality of capitalist production relations and bring material comfort and freedom to an alienated humanity. These ideas were to be developed later in *Eros and Civilization*.

In 1951-1952, he once more began lecturing at Columbia University in sociology. At the same time he was named senior fellow at Columbia's Russian Institute, occupying a similar position the following year at the Harvard Russian Research Center.[51] These research posts led to the publication of *Soviet Marxism* in 1958, the first part having been prepared at Columbia, and the second at Harvard with the aid of a Rockefeller Foundation grant.[52]

Because of the concentration of his activity, Marcuse was now no longer working directly with his Frankfurt friends. Possibly it explains why he alone of the Frankfurt group produced a booklength critique of Stalinism. But, as Arnason wrote, it may also have led to "a divergence on certain basic questions of critical theory."[53]

At the age of 56 Marcuse obtained his first full-time teaching post at Brandeis University in Waltham, Massachussetts,[54] where he taught philosophy and political science for eleven years. Brandeis, however, was primarily for undergraduates, as Andrew Hacker noted in *The New York Times Book Review.* Consequently, while there, Marcuse never confronted graduate students with his message.[55]

In 1955, again at age 56, Marcuse published his analysis of industrial society based on a neo-Freudian theory of repression, *Eros and Civilization.* In this work he endeavored to explain the role of the individual in social change. Even though the individual is increasingly engulfed by totalitarian society, nevertheless, by the use of his reason, he can hope to revive his rebellious subjectivity, which has its roots in an instinctual nature far older than the causes of the present situation. Habermas wrote, "Marcuse has a chiliastic trust in a revitalizing dynamic of instincts which works through history, finally breaks with history and leaves it behind as what then will appear as prehistory."[56]

Parenthetically, it should be noted here that Marcuse's second marriage took place on February 19, 1955, to Inge S. Werner. She was the widow of his friend Neumann, killed in a car accident in Switzerland on September 2, 1954.[57]

It was in 1956 that Marcuse first returned to Germany as an academic. He traveled to Frankfurt for the centenary celebrations of Freud's birth. While there, he delivered two lectures, "Progress and Freud's Theory of Instincts," and "Freedom and Freud's Theory of Instincts," which eventually appeared in English in *Five Lectures* in 1970. He was lecturing alongside such figures as Alexander, Balint, Erikson, and Spitz, and it was on this occasion that Habermas, later to become a friend, met him for the first time. Habermas explained that the anniversary made young German students realize that Freud was the father of a thriving scientific tradition. At the time, he noted, "Freud and Marx were 'dead dogs' and practically unknown at German universities."[58]

With *One-Dimensional Man* in 1964, Marcuse demonstrated that, "In the medium of technology, culture, politics, and the economy merge into an omnipresent system which swallows up or repulses all alternatives."[59] In fact, however, his intention was to denounce "repressive tolerance." The short work of this name, which still generates discussion today, formed part of the original manuscript of *One-Dimensional Man*, and was probably left out for lack of space.[60]

It was also in 1964, following his lecture on "Industrialization and Capitalism in the Work of Max Weber" at the fifteenth congress of German sociologists,[61] that violent reaction to Marcuse's views began to surface. Benjamin Nelson wrote a particularly harsh piece in *The New York Times Book Review*.[62] If we are to believe Raymond Aron, Nelson's reaction was justified by the fact that Marcuse's lecture "seemed to be inspired by a sort of fury against Max Weber, as though he were still alive and indomitable."[63] Marcuse made a point of replying to Nelson, saying that neither he nor the other participants had described Weber's work as a "total failure."[64] Actually, Marcuse paid tribute to Weber both at the beginning and end of his lecture. (Incidentally, the English translation, "Industrialization and Capitalism in Max Weber," published in *Negations* in 1968, is based on a revised 1965 German version. The French translation in *Culture et société* differs considerably.) In the last paragraph of the French version, Marcuse acknowledged with regard to Weber that "jusque dans ses limites, sa sociologie manifeste son éclatante supériorité sur toutes les sociologues qui se croient concrètes sous prétexte qu'elles refusent toute théorie." ("The whole of Weber's sociology demonstrates his brilliant superiority over all sociologists who, because they claim to reject theory entirely, consider themselves concrete.")[65] Similarly, he made a point of stating early in the lecture that: "This authentic concretion is the result of Weber's mastery of an immense material, of scholarship that seems unimaginable today, of knowledge that can afford to be absract because it can distinguish the essential from the inessential and reality from appearance."[66]

In 1965, in his sixty-seventh year, Marcuse was obliged to leave Brandeis after taking a public stand against its president, the historian Abram L. Sachar, who had founded the university twenty-two years earlier. As one of Marcuse's students that year tells it, a well-known anthropologist, Kathleen Aberle, said to the students one day, "Viva Fidel! Kennedy to hell!"[67] Sachar disapproved of such statements, fearing the university would be labeled Marxist. Marcuse, in what was probably the most important political act of his career, publicly opposed Sachar. "When I came to this country in the Thirties," he said, "there was a spirit of hope in the air. Now I detect a militarism and a repression that calls to mind the terror of Nazi Germany."[68] In May, Marcuse accepted an offer from the University of California at San Diego, where he was to end his teaching career after becoming a world-famous figure.

The Boston period had produced three of Marcuse's principal works as well as the German edition of collected essays that later appeared in *Five Lectures* and *Negations*. The message that was emerging was clear: it was imperative to develop an increasingly utopian form of thought in opposition to the status quo,[69] since total liberation would be possible if the forces of opposition were not so powerful.[70]

The year 1967 was marked by Marcuse's visit to the Free University in West Berlin. There he gave two highly publicized lectures, later to be published in English as "The End of Utopia" and "The Problem of Violence and the Radical Opposition," and he took part in three debates. His image as a prophet of revolution was in the making. For the time being, however, he was back in the city of his birth, "where, as a young man, he listened to Karl Liebknecht and Rosa Luxemburg," reported Melvin J. Lasky, who vividly described the atmosphere of these visits in the review *Preuves*.[71]

Debate centered on the dilemma of reform or revolution. As a student explained to Lasky, Marcuse taught them that the whole system was breaking down, that everything must be changed, and that revolution was the only way out. Here was the theorist confronting an assembly of practical revolutionaries, eager to hear what he would say next. The lecture was punctuated by shouts from the audience.

Not long after this came "the events of May '68," as the student occupation of the University of Paris has come to be called. Marcuse's name was linked to the events, and in April *The Times* of London asked, "Who is Henry Marcuse?" Who indeed? His correct Christian name was unknown, and yet the world press placed him beside Marx and Mao as one of the trinity looked to by young radicals, because he gave them a critical analysis of the system they were defying. Recalling his July 1967 visit to the Free University of West Berlin, *The Times* pointed out that although Marcuse supplied a theoretical basis for the student protest movement, members of the latter were disappointed by their mentor's negative theory, and reproached him for his lack of practical advice. One student disapproved of his cultural pessimism because it did not offer any concrete way of carrying out the revolution.[72]

While Marcuse did not go so far as to claim that his philosophy had established a link with practice, he thought that a Marxist philosopher like himself "participates in practice, at least to the extent that he takes a clear position on political questions, that he participates in demonstrations and in certain cases in the occupation of buildings, etc."[73] Marcuse actually took part in at least one sit-in of a San Diego building.[74]

On June 13, 1968, Harry L. Foster, a founding member of the American Legion in 1919, pushed a resolution through a Legion committee asking Governor Ronald Reagan to hold an inquiry into Dr. Marcuse, claiming that the latter wanted to bring Rudi Dutschke to San Diego. It is true that in Germany Dutschke had used Marcuse's name as a reference.[75] But "in reality, Dutschke intended to come to the United States for treatment at a Boston hospital."[76] Foster feared trouble on the campus. *The Union*, a San Diego newspaper, published an editorial stating that Marcuse had invited Dutschke. In the course of a single night, a little more than a dozen people contributed a $20,000 fund to buy out Marcuse's 1969-1970 contract. The University of California rejected the offer, however. Chancellor William McGill spoke to several groups, explaining how a university functions and pointing out the difference between theory and action. In his opinion "the Marcuse furor is just one facet of widespread anti-university sentiment transcending California's boundaries. Dr. Marcuse calls himself an analyst of society. He doesn't advocate the violent overthrow of the government."[77] And so, despite this campaign, Marcuse kept his post for another year.[78] But the storm was gathering.

Marcuse received a letter dated July 1, 1968, apparently from the Ku Klux Klan. It read: "You are a dirty Communist dog. You have 72 hours to leave the United States or you will be killed." On July 3, following an anonymous call, he had his telephone disconnected. On the July 4, after talking it over with his colleagues, he left home early in the morning with his wife.[79] Incidentally, a local newspaper had reported the threat, giving his full home address.[80] *The Times* of July 12 mentioned the disappearance, but added that the chairman of the philosophy department was in touch with him and had stated that Professor Marcuse had never tried to indoctrinate students, that he was probably the most popular professor on campus, and that he had never hidden the fact that he was Marxist. *The Saturday Evening Post* of Philadelphia described the event in detail,[81] and Edmund Stillman in *Horizon* compared it to Trotsky's last days in exile.[82]

The *drugstorisation* of Marcuse, as the French called it, was in full swing.[83] Comic strips,[84] plays,[85] posters,[86] crosswords,[87] and films[88] were made about him. He left "the groves of Academe to become a political slogan, embodying a whole current of ideas that guided an entire generation."[89] But Marcuse was still *Cet inconnu*—"This Unknown"—as *La Nef* of March 1969 described him in a subtitle.

It was in 1969 that Marcuse reconfirmed his support, encouragement, and hope for the student movement in *An Essay on Liberation*. In January François Perroux introduced Marcuse to his students at the College de France.[90] In a book based on the course, Perroux wrote that "Marcuse does not seem inclined toward an anarchist utopia."[91] And yet, in an exclusive interview with Louis Wiznitzer published in the Montreal *La Presse*, Marcuse, when asked about the possibility of "redefining socialism," replied: "It has been said of the May revolution that it was 'surrealistic,' utopian. That's right, and it's a good thing. . . ." (L.W.): "They've been criticized for being anarchists?" Marcuse: "That's right, and it's a good thing. Their anarchistic acts force the government to use brutal means of repression, thereby weakening society's *laissez-faire* ethics, reducing its effectiveness, and creating a climate of indifference [to authority]."[92]

In February, further pressure for Marcuse's resignation arose in the form of "a demand by Mr. John Stull, a Republican member of the state assembly, that they dismiss Dr. Herbert Marcuse, the theoretician of the student revolt, from his chair in San Diego. Governor Reagan has said that Dr. Marcuse's position as a state employee 'makes no sense.' "[93] In the fall of 1970 his contract was not renewed.[94]

Pope Paul VI, addressing thousands of pilgrims during his weekly audience on October 1, 1969, spoke out against the unbridled and disgusting expression of eroticism, mentioning

Freud and Marcuse together. "In this sad phenomenon . . . ," he said, "we find the theory that opens the way to license cloaked as liberty, and to the aberration of instincts called liberation."[95]

The world press described Marcuse as the prophet and guru of the New Left. But in fact Marcuse's career was above all that of a teacher. What, then, did people think of his courses in social and political philosophy? Michael Horowitz, who took a course in modern political theory during Marcuse's last year at Brandeis, quoted him as follows: "In the classroom I believe in only one power—faculty power. When we were students in Berlin, we never dictated to our professors, we listened to them!"[96] It may come as a surprise to learn that while Marcuse supported and encouraged student protest, he refused to allow protest in his classes. And yet he is reputed always to have been very attentive and perhaps even indulgent toward his students. According to Horowitz, sometimes Marxists and liberals would argue until the janitor came to complain. As for exams, Horowitz pointed out that there was no use taking them unless you could discuss Kant. Marcuse, he said, felt that "there is a certain amount of material that every intelligent person should learn—the basics of history, economics, psychology, philosophy, and so on."[97]

It is worth noting, however, that when Marcuse referred to history he nearly always went back to the Greeks of the sixteenth century B.C., as though nothing had happened since. As for economics, it is astonishing to learn from someone as well-known in the field as Allen Newman that Marcuse was ignored by economists generally.[98] But it is perhaps Marcuse's approach to all these fields that makes him so original. One may exclaim, as Horowitz did, "Poor Marcuse. Even in his popularity, he is out of step with the youth he seeks to guide." Yet the fact remains that in the Boston area Marcuse became "so popular that a newly endowed chair was named for him."[99] This popularity continued in California where, according to Sol Stern, Marcuse taught the classics of Western political thought in a setting of palm trees, beside sunny beaches where the students spent their afternoons surfing. "Marcuse has the unique talent," he wrote, "of making Kant, Hegel, and Marx seem relevant to a student body that looks like the cast of one of Hollywood's teen-age beach movies."[100]

Jean-Michel Palmier also noted Marcuse's talent for getting through to people: "Those students or professors who met him, particularly while he was teaching at Paris VIII (Vincennes) in May 1974, were struck by his enthusiasm, his generosity, and his simplicity."[101]

Among Marcuse's best known students were Angela Davis, Paul Piccone, Jeremy J. Shapiro, Trent Shroyer, Shierry Weber, William Leiss, Erica Sherover, and John David Ober.[102] The last three wrote an analysis of Marcuse as a teacher,[103] in which they stated, "The essential element of Marcuse's teaching is that knowledge is *partisan*."[104] This is because "Marcuse insists that in its origins and intentions knowledge (in the strictest sense: philosophy) was highly *subversive* of the established values and institutions."[105]

However if, in theory, knowledge must be partisan and subversive, does it follow that practical action must be violent? There is no easy answer. Raymond Aron, for example, reported the following conversation with Marcuse: "I said to him: 'Actually your philosophy is violence in order to achieve a completely pacified society.' He replied, 'That's it exactly.' "[106] On the other hand, the author of a short *Time* article reported a private conversation with Marcuse, in which the latter conceded that in the United States it might be possible to escape repression without a violent revolution.[107] In the final analysis, such ambiguity is perhaps inherent in any concept of revolution. In any case, this theoretical ambiguity was directly reflected in Marcuse's life. In fact, he described himself as a traitor to the cause—"a fink."[108] His dilemma was that while he believed everything to be bad and in need of change, he also felt that some American universities might enable "the movement" to reach its goals within existing institutions.

The 1977 *Année politique, économique, sociale et diplomatique en France* referred to September as a month of violence.[109] In Bonn on September 5, the Red Army Faction (or Baader-Meinhof gang) kidnapped and executed Hans Martin Schleyer, president of the West German federations of management and industry. International public opinion was aroused, and the media launched into a heated discussion. The German federal government was accused by some of indecisiveness, and by others of driving the powerless extreme left to despair and terrorism. Writer Heinrich Böll, Rudi Dutschke,[110] and Marcuse,[111] three figures well-known in West Germany as sympathetic to the New Left, publicly disavowed the terrorists. Dutschke and Marcuse had met on August 4 at the funeral of Ernst Bloch, and now their names were linked once again. Rudi Dutschke considered that each violent act increasingly obscured the revolutionary struggle. Marcuse's position appeared more complex. He saw it as a question of revolutionary morality, in the sense that no action is justifiable unless it has a chance of succeeding. Moreover, "By personalizing the struggle, the terrorists must be held accountable and judged for their actions. Those representatives of capital whom the terrorists have chosen as their victims are themselves responsible for capitalism—just as Hitler and Himmler were responsible for the concentration camps. This means that the victims of terror are not innocent—but their guilt can only be expiated through the abolition of capitalism itself."[112]

On the evening of August 29, 1979, Marcuse died of a stroke at Starnberg in West Germany. He was 81. In accordance with his last wishes, his body was cremated. Marcuse had remained active, and was actually in Germany at the invitation of the Max Planck Institute. He had given what was to be his last public lecture on May 17 at the annual Romergespräche, a symposium organized by the city of Frankfurt.[113]

Will Marcuse's work endure? His theories have been subject to so many attacks that one cannot help wondering whether they will continue to stimulate interest. One thing is certain: to read Marcuse is to reflect. This, in itself, is reason enough to try to discern what makes his writings so original. Even so, it does not explain the Marcuse phenomenon. His popularity after the events of 1968 was so great that even those who had never read his work were interested in him. How had he become so famous? And above all, what real expectations were (or still are) fulfilled by Marcuse's analysis of our society? Is there some old or new current of thought for which Marcuse became—for a time at least—the principle exponent?

In the years following World War I, both Marxists and psychoanalysts were looking for ways to unite the two currents of thought which they represented. This search was dubbed "Freudo-Marxism."[114] William Reich seems to have spearheaded the movement, as demonstrated in his 1929 essay on *Dialectical Materialism and Psychoanalysis*.[115] It is possible to link

Reich and Marcuse in several ways,[116] as André Nicolas has done in studies on both these writers.[117] It was not only Marcuse, however, but most of the Frankfurt School that helped build Freudo-Marxist theory, notably Erich Fromm, at one time connected to the Institute for Social Research.[118] Despite the fact that they were working in the same direction, Fromm nevertheless delivered himself of some harsh judgments. "Marcuse is essentially an example of an alienated intellectual who presents his personal despair as a theory of radicalism," said Fromm. "It is a naïve, cerebral daydream, essentially irrational, unrealistic, and lacking love of life."[119] Fromm was not the only one who felt this way. François Châtelet, for example, stated that when one dreams of a great Freudo-Marxist synthesis, as Marcuse did, "one's writing can only be platitudinous nonsense or pure speculation."[120] Actually, the pessimistic archeology of Freud and the historical optimism of Marx reflect basic positions that are too opposed for genuine synthesis. If we agree with Fromm and Châtelet, then the importance of Marcuse must lie elsewhere. It seems to me that André Nicolas is correct in his view that "Marcuse's three major conceptual spaces" are "the works of Hegel, Marx, and Freud,"[121] but that he is "a heretic" in their regard.[122]

In my opinion, Marcuse's contribution is to be found in the Frankfurt School. Although French interest in this school has emerged later than in other countries, no one who has read Martin Jay's study published in 1973 can doubt its significance.[123] We can forgive André Clair for having omitted any mention of critical theory, virtually the school's trademark, in his 1969 analysis of Marcuse's work, "Réflexions et interrogations sur les fondements de l'oeuvre,"[124] since he did emphasize utopia, one of the key ideas of this theory. It is harder to understand why Jean-Marie Vincent, in his 1976 book on *La Théorie critique de l'école de Frankfort*, should decide to exclude all reference to Marcuse.[125] Fortunately, Gérard Raulet has made good this omission in his 1978 *Marxisme et théorie critique*.[126] Generally speaking, however, the French have judged Marcuse's work very severely. Some have deemed it *un massacre pour des bagatelles*—a tempest in a teapot.[127] Jules Monnerot devoted one of the 700 pages of his *Sociologie de la révolution*, a twentieth-century study, to describing Marcuse as "a mediocre thinker."[128] Raymond Ruyer saw "non-repressive civilization" as "philosophical demagoguery."[129] Jacques Ellul considered Marcuse's thinking "completely confused and inarticulate."[130] Julien Freund wrote that Marcusian sociology "ceases to be a science in which the object is the analysis of existing or past concrete societies, and becomes the pretext for a rhetoric in which aggressive language hides ignorance."[131] Pierre Masset concluded his analysis of *La Pensée de Herbert Marcuse* by stating that, "in the end, the answer he brings to the problems of our time is . . . not only inadequate or empty, but false and dangerous."[132] Even François Perroux, while sympathetic and friendly in his approach,[133] felt that people could be excused for regarding the struggle for "pacified existence" as "a recipe for bored petits-bourgeois."[134]

René Viénet, who worked with several members of the international situationist movement and the Groupe des Enragés, contended that "Marcusian *ideology*, already in disrepute, was tacked onto the movement."[135] In Russia, Marcuse's "Western delirium," as Vadim Delaunay called it,[136] was denounced by Motroshilova, a member of the Moscow Philosophy Institute, as well as by Zamoshkin, president of the USSR Academy of Science,[137] and Yuri Zhukov, editor of *Pravda*.[138] Alasdair MacIntyre in England wrote, "Almost all of Marcuse's key positions are false,"[139] and concluded, "Marcuse has produced a theory that . . . invokes the great names of freedom and reason while betraying their substance at every important point."[140] Without overstating the case, it seems clear that Marcuse attracted attention, not despite his weaknesses, but often because of them. He himself admitted his weaknesses. Caught between his desire to express his pessimism about the revolution on the one hand, and to defend his utopian optimism on the other, he found himself in an awkward if not ambiguous position. But, as Sidney Lipshires so aptly remarked, "the very ambiguity of his position in regard to the prospects for revolution mirrors for us (and for the historian of the future) the revolutionary utopianism of our times."[141] This is reason enough to study Marcuse and the current of thought to which he adhered.

It is my contention that the twentieth century has witnessed the renaissance, from a new perspective, of a current of thought that has probably always been with us, although its sudden resurgence may have been unexpected. Utopia seeks to liberate desire and the world of imagination. For Freud, ours is the century of dreams; he deciphered their meaning and gave us the key. Even so, the lure of the unknown is still strong. The all-pervading rationalism of science and technology seems to stimulate a compensatory urge at the primitive levels of the psyche. Nostalgia for the wilderness appears to go hand in hand with the "technetronic revolution." In fact, technological progress has apparently extended the realm of dreams into a new space—that of "day-dreams," as Ernst Bloch put it. If this is indeed the case, we need to rethink the links that have been forged between utopia and revolution. This is exactly what Marcuse did, to the point of meriting, rightly or wrongly, the title of prophet of the New Left.

Will Marcuse's revolutionary spirit survive? The last years in San Diego before his death in 1979 were essentially taken up with defending the spirit of utopian revolution, not to say revolutionarism. "The End of Utopia," originally published in 1967, and the 1969 *Essay on Liberation* provided a critique of the new affluence and the student New Left. *Counterrevolution and Revolt* in 1972 showed the capitalist system working for institutionalization of the counterrevolution in order to eradicate the first symptoms of a world-wide revolutionary movement. Marcuse criticized those who thought that production relations alone were responsible for the status quo. All man's relations with nature, with man, and with his future must be taken into account. He opposed the ritualization of revolutionary theory, and developed the theory of a new revolutionary sensitivity in nature, politics, and art. In 1975, the three lectures collected in *Actuels* took such ideas even further. Finally, in 1977, came his philosophical testament, *The Aesthetic Dimension*, dealing with the possibility of revolutionary art.

How far have Marcuse's ideas entered the stream of philosophical discussion? English-language writers have maintained a fairly constant and regular interest in his work. The French have probably absorbed a few of his ideas through Habermas, and Gérard Raulet seems to be working in this direction. In 1968, German writers immediately appeared to grasp the fact that Marcuse was a utopian thinker. This can be seen in the articles of Gerd-Klaus Kaltenbrunner and Maria Szecsi, for example.[142] Nothing seems to have appeared in China, apparently because he is a forbidden subject for publication. The same is true of Russia, although the young intelligentsia is inspired by his work, as shown by the public demonstration involving 200 young people outside the Kazan Cathedral on December 5, 1978.[143] Led by 20-year-old Aleksander and 19-year-old Arkady Tourkov, the group known as the "Leningrad School" (in imitation of the Frankfurt School), believes that in the USSR the opposition must do away with the bureaucratic class through a revolutionary process in which the working class is to be led by the intelligentsia. The consequence has been a considerable amount of published material denouncing Marcuse, a negative but nonetheless real testimony to the presence of his ideas.[144]

II

The Forerunners of Marcuse's Utopia

It is only by studying the long history of utopia, from Plato to Thomas Münzer, from More to Fourier and Marx, that we can appreciate the real significance of the utopian theses in Eros and Civilization.[1]

So voluminous is utopian literature that a single lifetime would not suffice to read and analyze it all. Henri Desroche, in an article with the tongue-in-cheek title, "A Small Utopian Library," listed a large number of works that were themselves bibliographies of the thousands of literary utopias.[2] As Alexander Cioranescu pointed out, the subject of utopia has in turn produced an abundance of critical works that may well outnumber the utopias themselves.[3] Given this plethora of writing, it seems pointless to look for one definition of all the phenomena covered by the term "utopia." The truth of this statement is borne out by studies such as those by Paul Ricoeur, Lyman Tower Sargent, Paul Swada, and especially by utopian experts such as Frank E. Manuel and his wife Fritzie P. Manuel.[4] Marcuse himself professed to be not much interested in "the semantics of the term Utopianism," remarking that, "as the word loses more and more of its traditional content, it becomes an instrument of political defamation."[5] He did not make an issue of it, however. For example, in a conversation with Raymond Aron he said simply, "You may call me utopian."[6]

Actually, most writers are content with a definition that suits their purpose, and there seems little reason to approve or condemn utopian theory out of hand on purely theoretical grounds. One must remember that where Marcuse is concerned, each time he spoke of utopia he presupposed "the end of utopia," as demonstrated by his definition of "utopian" in *An Essay on Liberation*: "The actual evolution of contemporary societies deprives 'utopia' of its traditional unreal content: what it denounced as 'utopian' is no longer that which has 'no place' and cannot have any place in the historical universe, but rather that which is blocked from coming about by the power of the established societies."[7] In the mid-twentieth century, he explained, utopia is only an impossible dream for theorists who use the concept "to denounce certain socio-historical possibilities."[8] This is why Marcuse offered us a "transcendent project" or a project in which utopia is not seen as a threat. He included himself in the long list of utopians stretching from Plato and antiquity to the eighteenth-century modernity of Rousseau, Babeuf, and Schiller. For him, the important figures in the nineteenth century were Fourier, Bakunin, and Marx, and in the twentieth, Luxemburg and Mannheim.

History books make much of the social utopia connected with Platonic theory, and it is true that Plato can be thought of as the precursor of the utopians in that he inspired them. But Plato was not the first utopian. The *Republic* of his predecessor, Antisthenes the Cynic, offered a world without private property established without violence. Plato borrowed heavily from the urbanist utopia of Hippodamus of Miletus, mainly with regard to the division of social classes. However, it is not enough simply to define the Platonic utopia in terms of its socialist aspect, or to describe "The Egalitarian Utopias of the Hellenic Era," as Mossé did.[9] For the purpose of this study, it would be more meaningful to find some other perspective, equally important as socialism, from which to demonstrate the originality of utopian thought in relation to socialist theory. We can do this by looking at Plato's political philosophy as a whole.

The Platonic utopia can be seen from at least three different angles. Ciorenescu wrote: "There are utopian characteristics—or characteristics viewed as utopian—which he may well have invented in the myth of Atlantis, as well as in his abstract, ideal republic. The two images are not identical, however."[10] Furthermore, some of the characteristics of the *Laws* have been altered in the light of the *Republic*.

In the first place, the main characteristics of the utopian genre are discernible in the myth of Atlantis. As described in the dialogues of *Timaeus* and *Critias*, this island, along with many others, formed part of a large and wonderful empire that existed in the distant past. Solon supposedly told the story of Atlantis to the grandfather of Critias after hearing it from an old Egyptian priest.

Secondly, we can see the spirit of utopia or the passion for perfection operating in the search for "a perfect State," although Plato warned, "You must not insist on my proving that the actual State will in every respect coincide with the ideal."[11] This is the pursuit of perfection demonstrated by Ernst Bloch, "the will to seek an ideal world that always pervades the utopian consciousness"[12] and characterizes "the day-dream."[13]

In the third place, the *Laws* can virtually be analyzed from the standpoint of a working utopia, given the precise nature of Plato's instructions with reference to the *Republic*, designed to make his laws more easily applicable. It is illuminating to note that Plato traveled to Syracuse three times, as the famous "Letter VII" tells us, to convince Dion of Syracuse to apply his ideas. Did he intend to realize utopia? Or ought we to make a distinction between the young and the old Plato, the better to understand the debate on utopia and reality?

Let us take the single aspect of education, so central to Hellenic civilization, as Henri-Irénée Marrou demonstrated.[14] It may well have had a utopian tradition, a possibility explored by Henri Desroche.[15]

We can formulate the question in the following terms: is there a significant relation between education and utopia? Etymologically speaking, education is supposed to bring the individual out into the world, whereas utopia implies a transition to another world. The fundamental question in education is whether, in learning from those who preceded us, we perpetuate visions of the past or create a new future. Similarly, one of the basic problems of utopia is that when we attempt to take it seriously, it is difficult to know whether it represents anticipation of the future or simply nostalgia for the past.[16] With Plato, both points of view seem defensible. For example, his view of ancient Athens as superior to the Athens of his day was considered nostalgic by Raymond Trousson.[17] On the other hand, Marrou held that not everything in Plato was purely utopian, and that the theory of education in particular gave rise to anticipation.[18] Since utopias almost always imply both anticipation and nostalgia, I do not propose to settle the debate within the confines of this work. The question I have in mind is the following: can culture generally, and education in particular, bridge the gap between reality and utopia?

In comparing the *Republic* and *Laws*, it becomes clear that education was the means by which Plato intended to realize his utopia. "Education," Ruyer wrote, "which was one of Plato's constant preoccupations, has a very different meaning in the *Laws* as compared to the *Republic*."[19]

In the *Republic*, Plato entrusted the application of his political ideal to the philosophers. In the *Laws*, however, he gave a detailed description of the best possible regulations for a Greek city of his time. As with most utopians, the legislators' main concern was education. According to Ruyer, this preoccupation demonstrated their visible anxiety "to work on an entirely new generation."[20] It is as though they wanted to start from scratch. The end of Book VII in the *Republic* makes it clear: "They will begin by sending out into the country all the inhabitants of the city who are more than ten years old, and will take possession of their children, who will be unaffected by the habits of their parents; these they will train in their own habits and laws, which will be such as we have described."[21] But why propose a system of education that denies parents the right to educate their children? It is inconsistent. As Molnar pointed out, "Granted that this is a necessity *once*, when the great break between the old and new is effected; but if the new product is reliable from the point of view of utopian cohesion, then the parents of the future should be trusted to bring up their offspring in the new spirit in which they themselves were educated."[22]

Plato seemed undeterred by this contradiction, and in fact pushed his idea much further. In *The Statesman*, he allowed the rulers of a "true political regime" to kill or exile each other: "Or if they should effect a wholesome purgation of the state by executions or sentences of banishment, or again, diminish its numbers by sending out colonists, as a hive of bees might a swarm, or swell them by bestowing the franchise on immigrants introduced from abroad, so long as they only preserve the state and do all they may to make it better than they found it, by the application of *science* and *justice*, we must still insist that the only true constitution is that of such a time, founded on such principles."[23] In other words, it is dictatorship, along with education, that will assure the transition to utopia.

All this leads me to make three observations. As with other utopian thinkers, the dominant characteristic of Plato's utopian education resides in its proposal of a system of education destined to change both contemporary and future man, as Molnar observed. He also noted that "utopians prefer to work with the young."[24] (We will see a further instance of this with Marcuse.) Finally, Plato's innumerable directives to the rulers of his ideal republic, covering everything from birth control to literary censorship, clearly laid him open to charges of totalitarianism. Consequently, the idea of an "educational dictatorship," taken up by Rousseau in the form of compulsory education toward freedom, should have been viewed with far greater skepticism by Marcuse.

Julien Freund was right in remarking that the phrase "educational dictatorship" did not slip into Marcuse's writing by accident, but appeared in most of his work.[25] Actually, Marcuse claimed that "the answer to Plato's educational dictatorship is the democratic educational dictatorship of free men."[26] He put the following question: "Is there any alternative other than the dictatorship of an 'elite' over the people?"[27] He subsequently answered it, asserting that "The alternative to the established semi-democratic process is *not* a dictatorship or elite, no matter how intellectual and intelligent, but the struggle for a real democracy."[28] Was this simply an escape into abstraction? Or had Marcuse a specific plan of action for this struggle? He attempted to explain himself on this subject at least three times.

During a 1972 debate, Raymond Aron spoke from his experience of communism as it exists in the Soviet Union, and of liberalism as the guardian of individual safety and freedom. Marcuse replied with arguments based on communism as it ought to be, and defined democratic communism as "a society in which the individuals collectively determine the organization and the direction of the economic and political life, and in which each individual has an equal opportunity to develop his or her individual needs."[29] Aron considered this explanation too abstract, and asked him to use concrete terms. Marcuse then added that he would call on general assemblies, to be held in factories, villages, farms, and residential areas, both locally and regionally, for the purpose of naming delegates who "would be revocable—recallable at any moment." Aron felt that this was hardly original; Lenin had already talked of it, and furthermore, it had been tried and had failed. The dialogue continued as follows:

> Marcuse: . . . the fact that something failed once. . . .
> Aron: No, twenty times, twenty times, not once.
> Marcuse: No, no, no, let's agree on twelve times. If it failed twelve times, that doesn't mean that the thirteenth time it may not succeed. . . .
> Aron: It's an argument in favor of the ideal. If it failed twelve times, then there are some reasons for that.
> Marcuse: No. If for a thousand years men couldn't think of a democratic—and create a democratic—society, that doesn't mean that there must be a reason that it will always fail.[30]

But while waiting for his democratic communism to materialize, what did Marcuse suggest? He adopted the same perspective as Plato, who was ready to kill or banish various people, and Rousseau, who, had he been king of Negritia (the Sudan), would have built gallows on the frontiers, either to hang everyone wanting to escape to countries ruined by civilization, or conversely to execute all the civilized people trying to enter.[31] Marcuse thus placed himself in the long tradition of revolutionary dictatorship. Instead of dictatorship of the proletariat, he spoke of "educational dictatorship," but this only differed from the former in terms of its justification, as Ljubomir Tadić explained.[32] Under present conditions of civilization, Marcuse suggested educating "liberation specialists" to implement educational dictatorship. During a 1968 debate on ethics and politics, he replied explicitly to Professor Lowenthal: "There is a technique of liberation, a technology of liberation which must be learned. It is our duty to contribute to augmenting the number of these specialists and reinforcing their position."[33] This "moral obligation" connected with the "idea of a preparatory educational dictatorship," was analyzed by Marcuse in *Repressive Tolerance*. His principle was to grant freedom of thought to all who agreed with him, and deny it to others on the ground that they used *bad* violence, whereas he proposed *good* violence—violence that would lead to man's liberation.[34]

Marcuse had not said his last word on the subject, however. In a 1978 interview published in *Telos*, when pressed by repeated questions from Jürgen Habermas, he made several avowals. His remarks were surprising, to say the least. Once again he was led to comment on the following statement from *Eros and Civilization* published in 1955: "From Plato to Rousseau, the only honest answer is the idea of an educational dictatorship, exercised by those who are supposed to have acquired knowledge of the real Good."[35] What Marcuse now said was: "Today I wouldn't talk about educational dictatorship. The passage you cited was intentionally written for purposes of provocation. Perhaps educational dictatorship within democracy, but not simply educational dictatorship period."[36] Perhaps, as Jean Roy remarked in a 1979 article, this was a rather facile remark, since Marcuse was claiming in retrospect that he was not serious in constructing his notion of repressive tolerance.[37] At the time, however, his major critic, David Spitz, and his friends on the magazine *Dissent*, reacted very unfavorably.[38] It is difficult to believe that Marcuse meant what he said in 1978. He apparently wanted to reply to Spitz, but nothing came of it.

To what extent, then, can we credit Marcuse's thought? We can only take note of the fact that, as he himself said, his thought is provocative, partisan, subversive, and revolutionary, and that different ways of envisaging the transition to the perfect society add up to the same thing, whether we are talking of planned revolution, unavoidable catastrophe, or the kind of education that will emerge when humanity has attained a sufficient degree of maturity. We can only hope for the millenium foreshadowed in the utopian tradition, particularly that of the eighteenth century, when the word "utopia" became a common noun that gained immediate popularity.

During the eighteenth century, utopia continued to refer to the limited meaning of an imaginary island, with Sir Thomas More's island of Utopia remaining the paradigm. In a larger sense, however, it expanded to include a universal vision of social life, radically opposed to existing social reality and its system of values. Utopia came to represent an awareness of rupture between social reality as it ought to be, and as it was. And, finally, it became the rejection of social reform to the extent that it represented a desire to begin *ex nihilo*. Utopia "ceased to be a mental exercise involving a lateral possible world, and became an exercise involving an ulterior, probable world," in Trousson's words.[39] In this sense, Ruyer's definition of the "utopian mode" as "a mental exercise on a lateral possibility" was too limited.[40] Marcuse's interest in Rousseau, Babeuf, and Schiller—an interest in "the classical century of utopia," as Ruyer called it—can be better understood in relation to the radically expanded eighteenth-century meaning of utopia.[41]

Marcuse occasionally criticized Rousseau explicitly,[42] but he also used him to support argument,[43] although this was most often implicit rather than explicit. Julien Freund compared the mentality of the eighteenth century in general, and of Rousseau in particular, to that of Marcuse.[44] This comparison was taken even further by Jean-Marie Benoist from the standpoint of structuralist, linguistic philosophy,[45] in order to indulge in what Birou saw as a vicious critique of Marcuse.[46] It is my view that Rousseau and Marcuse were aware of their utopian outlook, even if only to reject it, as in the case of Rousseau, who commented wryly on the furor over one of his works: "Well, sir, if I had merely constructed a System, you may be sure no one would have said anything. People were quite content to consign *The Social Contract*, along with Plato's *Republic*, *Utopia*, and *Sévarambes* to the land of chimeras."[47] Marcuse demonstrated his awareness by accepting the utopia, inasmuch as it represented a means of going beyond advanced industrial society: "The utopia of the man who plays has a real basis in the degree of well-being already attained through productivity. To approach this utopia, we need to formulate the idea of a liberating humanism: . . . a conversion of productivity by the suppression of all destructive and parasitic production; the rebuilding of cities . . . ; the revival of nature . . . ; the limitation of population growth are the necessary conditions for a humane society."[48]

This utopian perspective, whether acknowledged or not, inevitably involves an essentially ambiguous question, if we are right in assuming that all utopias imply a basic ambiguity. Interestingly enough, we find the same question in Rousseau's *Social Contract*: "Where shall we find a form of association which will defend and protect with the whole common force the person and property of each associate, and by which every person, while uniting himself with all, shall obey only himself and remain as free as before?"[49] Similarly, in the conclusion to *One-Dimensional Man*, Marcuse asked: "How can the administered individuals . . . liberate themselves from themselves as well as from their masters? How is it even thinkable that the vicious circle be broken?"[50] But can either philosopher overcome the contradiction or break out of the vicious circle? It seems not, since Rousseau admitted "that men should be, before the formation of laws, what those laws alone can make them,"[51] and since Marcuse considered "the greatest difficulty in the matter" to be the fact that, "for new revolutionary needs to develop, the mechanisms that reproduce the old needs must be abolished. In order for the mechanisms to be abolished, there must first be a need to abolish them. That is the circle in which we are placed, and I do not know how to get out of it."[52] Yet both Rousseau and Marcuse insisted on the same hypothetical solution, or—as Marcuse expressed it—on "Rousseau's revolutionary principle of compulsory education toward freedom."[53] I emphasize the word "hypothetical," because for Marcuse "this 'if' is essential,"[54] and for Rousseau there were only "hypothetical and conditional arguments"[55] in this domain. Actually, there is nothing surprising in all this, since both started from the same premise. Rousseau stated early in his "Discourse on the Origin of Inequality": "Let us begin by setting aside all the facts."[56] Marcuse proposed "to break the power of facts over the world, and to speak a language which was not the language of those who establish, enforce, and benefit from the facts."[57]

The method of both philosophers is therefore similar. The same is true of their intention in terms of the possible and the impossible. Both felt that all things could be measured in terms of the possible, Rousseau wanting to take "men such as they are, and laws such as they may be made,"[58] and Marcuse seeking the "interpretation of that-which-is in terms of that-which-is-not."[59] But they also felt that all things could be measured in terms of the impossible, with Rousseau interested in "changing human nature, to to speak,"[60] and Marcuse believing that no social change is valid "unless we have something that could almost be called a change in human nature,"[61] as well as stating that "a new experience of being would change the human existence in its entirety."[62]

All in all, Rousseau and Marcuse conceived a project for human communal life with no methodical provision for realizing it, as Mühlmann stated in his definition of the utopian outlook.[63] Freund considered it enlightened despotism, summed up by a German socialist with the typical formula: "To prove the truth of our doctrine, we'll change human nature if necessary."[64] This point of view has its drawbacks, as Marcuse seemed to realize. This is why he cited Myrdal, for whom "the concept of nature" was a "cliché that functions just like every other political recommendation . . . when anyone, in some political question, wants to assert something without adducing proof of it."[65] Marcuse was not unduly concerned, however, remarking in 1978, in answer to a query by Heinz Lubasz, that "It's entirely possible for Rousseau to have said something sensible."[66] Perhaps he indicated his sympathetic understanding of Rousseau when he said in 1968, "In America we are entering a new 'Age of Enlightenment.' "[67]

Although the utopians of the Enlightenment, such as Morelly and Rousseau, might see the utopian city as being constructed outside of fact, there were others who insisted that utopia should have some impact on reality. Such was the case with Gracchus Babeuf. Like Thomas Munzer, Babeuf proposed utopia in action. He believed in direct democracy, and 1796 inaugurated an underground organization for which he was arrested. In 1797, a three-month trial began which confirmed "the failure of utopia in action," as Raymond Trousson put it.[68] Babeuf's failure did not matter, according to Marcuse's analysis of his *Defense*. Even if Babeuf could not transform his radical ideology into reality, it was nonetheless valid and "could be transmitted to future generations and serve as guide in the preparation for future struggles."[69] On Babeuf's theory, centered on notions of popular sovereignty and conspiracy, he commented, "Its historical significance far transcends the specific circumstances under which his trial took place."[70] What exactly was this special historical significance? We can get a more precise idea by looking at three points on which Babeuf and Marcuse concurred: the rejection of current democracy, the belief in ideal democracy, and the call to violence to establish direct democracy.

The rejection of existing democracy was recommended by Babeuf on the basis of the idea that the people are not necessarily sovereign because they have voted for their constitution and representatives. "The people might be misled; they might, 'with apparent freedom, have adopted a radically vicious Constitution.' "[71] Babeuf built his *Defense* on this notion, admitting the fact of conspiracy, but submitting that it was not a true conspiracy, since this could only be possible where direct democracy guaranteed the true interest of the people. Representative democracy did not guarantee this, said Babeuf; it only gave the people apparent sovereignty. As a result (to quote Marcuse's summary of Babeuf's arguments), "the establishment of democracy would mean subversion of the established democracy."[72] We can see that Marcuse shared this opinion from his remark that "democracy certainly has a future. But in my view it certainly does not have a present."[73] He made this statement when raising the question, as did Babeuf, of "whether the majority today is a free majority or not."[74] Both philosophers apparently felt it was not. This is why Maurice Cranston, speaking in almost Marcusian terms, was correct in saying that Marcuse shared with Babeuf "the belief that the political sentiments held by a misled, indoctrinated and ignorant populace are not to be regarded as the people's real will, and that the establishment of a 'real republic' involved acting (and writing) against the majority."[75]

But what criterion, what democratic ideal, can justify their condemnation of factual democracy? Here is what Marcuse found in Babeuf: "In theory, the criteria for the harmony of an established social order with the true interests of the people were the realization of the inalienable rights of man as stated in the 'ageless book of nature.' "[76]

What about Marcuse's criterion of ideal democracy? He acknowledged it in the following manner. Arthur M. Schlesinger, Jr., remarked to him that his position implied the concept of a golden age of democracy in which the majority is pure, totally free, and acts wisely. Marcuse replied: "If you want me to make it perfectly clear once and for all, I do admit such a democracy has never existed and does not exist in any society today. But I do believe that we can have it."[77] As Julien Freund rightly remarked, Babeuf and Marcuse were advocates of the revolution because they believed that "humanity has evolved enough to finally realize a form of society ruled by fraternity, justice, and happiness," and because they wished to eliminate the forces of evil that prevent "the realization of such an ideal society."[78]

But if the moment has at last come to realize ideal democracy, how are we to do it? Normally, the specific nature of the end governs the means. When it comes to changing human nature, however, there can be no middle course. There is only violence, which represses and humiliates man without changing him. Babeuf, as is well known, preached armed insurrection. Marcuse, for his part, stated emphatically that "the definition of democracy" must include "the forcible occupation of buildings and the invasion of private property," because this is "a part of the democratic process."[79]

In the final analysis, Babeuf and Marcuse wished to impose direct democracy from above, by forcing the ignorant populace to exercise "real" sovereignty. Occasionally, it seemed as though there was a divergence of views, such as in Marcuse's concluding remarks to the effect that "a theory and strategy which was quite unrealistic but not utopian in 1796 appears as utterly utopian today."[80] This was not, as some might think, a negative judgment of Babeuf's utopia. One has only to recall Marcuse's declared position on this point: "I would really like to confess to Utopia for the simple reason that nowadays the concept of Utopia has become meaningless. . . . There is actually nothing which rationally and with a good conscience we should despise and denounce as Utopian. We could actually do anything today. We could certainly have a rational society, and just *because* that is such a near possibility its actual realization is more "Utopian" than ever before; the whole force of the *status quo* is mobilized against it."[81] Basically, the more he believed in the possibility of realizing utopia, the more he was convinced that the ruling class opposed it and vice versa. This class was doing its best to hinder realization of a utopia that would eliminate it. But this resistance did not negate the ever-present possibility of realizing utopia, according to Marcuse.

As long as we are convinced of the need to realize utopia, its failure to materialize, whether in Babeuf's day or our own, only encourages expectation and even preparation. Marcuse considered that the best way to prepare for utopian realization was to look first for the possibility or tendency in the aesthetic domain. The reason was that, in his view, "*The utopian idea of aesthetic reality must be sustained to the point of ridicule necessarily associated with it today.*"[82] This is what he did, taking his inspiration from yet another eighteenth-century thinker, Schiller.

The great German writer and dramatist wanted to help bring about a better world through poetry. He used Kantian philosophy, which attempted to explore the preconditions of the status quo, in order to deduce the hypothetical preconditions for the emergence of a totally free human personality and a society of peaceable beings. For Schiller, the eighteenth-century hypothesis of harmony in nature was characterized by two essential and opposite factors: happiness, the goal of sensual man; and perfection, the goal of moral man.[83] To overcome the contradiction between the "sensuous impulse" (*Stofftrieb*) and the "form-impulse" (*Formtrieb*), Schiller posited the "play impulse" (*Spieltrieb*), which he saw as the basis of artistic activity in general. It would allow the development of freedom, with humanity no longer being artifically divided between instinct and reason.

Such was the context within which Marcuse worked from 1937 on, basing himself on a statement at the end of Schiller's second letter on the aesthetic education of man. "Schiller says that the 'political problem' of a better organization of society 'must take the path through the aesthetic realm, because it is through beauty that one arrives at freedom.' "[84] This statement was to become one of the major themes of *Eros and Civilization*, and it is in this context that we can understand how Marcuse arrived at the concept of "the aesthetic *ethos* which provides the common denominator of the aesthetic and political."[85] In his later years, Marcuse made it clear that he was still working along these lines. In a letter to Morton Schoolman on December 2, 1975, Marcuse said clearly that his philosophy was now principally directed toward the problems of art and aesthetics.[86]

What is the connection between art and utopia, therefore? Frederic Jameson, interpreting Schiller from a Marxist standpoint, expressed it in terms that apply equally well to Marcuse. "In art, consciousness prepares itself for a change in the world itself and at the same time learns to make demands on the real world which hasten that change: for the experience of the imaginary offers (in an imaginary mode) that total satisfaction of the personality and of Being in the light of which the real world stands condemned, in the light of which the Utopian idea, the revolutionary blueprint, may be conceived."[87] But an even greater understanding of all the resources of aesthetic utopia can be gained from the French social theorist, Charles Fourier, who exploited these resources to the full. Marcuse certainly had no hesitation in looking to him for guidance.

Who was Fourier? The question is still being asked, particularly since the edition of his complete works does not even contain all the books and pamphlets published during his lifetime, as Emile Lehouck pointed out in 1966.[88] Raymond Ruyer considered Fourier "a self-taught genius"[89] and "a likable maniac."[90] Lehouck felt that Fourier was at least as prolific as Hugo and Balzac, and that he outstripped them in sheer creativity.[91] Furthermore, not only did his work "herald and complete Marxism," it was a hundred years ahead of its time in propounding "the basis of psychoanalysis."[92] Raymond Trousson introduced Fourier with a quote from *Théorie des quatre mouvements* (1808) that seemed to indicate delusions of grandeur rather than genius. "I alone shall have overcome twenty centuries of political imbecility; present and future generations will owe the beginning of their immense happiness to none but me. . . . The book of destiny is mine; I have come to clear away political and moral cobwebs, and to construct the theory of universal harmony upon the ruins of the inexact sciences."[93]

What was Fourier's influence on Marcuse? Jean Lacroix wrote that "the real utopian philosopher of happiness in the nineteenth century was Charles Fourier, who identified 'Happiness and Harmony.' "[94] Marcuse's early work contained a similar identification. The basic link between Marcuse and Fourier was the search for total happiness in total freedom, both instinctual and political. This was demonstrated by Jean-Paul Thomas in his recent *Libération instinctuelle politique: Contribution fouriériste à Marcuse*.[95] Thomas showed the importance of aesthetics in Marcuse's critical theory, and this was exactly what Marcuse's reference to Fourier meant: an aesthetic commitment.

Marcuse tried to show that "the utopia of the man who plays has a real basis."[96] In *Eros and Civilization*, he based this argument on Schiller's "play impulse" aimed at beauty and freedom,[97] and on Fourier's "attractive labor."[98] Francis Hearn, in "Toward a Critical Theory of Play," attempted to develop a theory based on these ideas.[99] In social theory generally, he explained, there is no room for a serious analysis of play. Marcuse was the exception to the rule, because he considered play essential to the development of the individual and the human race. Play does not deny reality, but reinvigorates it by allowing people to look at it critically. In advanced industrial society, play tends to turn into inactivity or idleness, allowing us to escape from society rather than making us aware of what it really is. The Paris student protest of May 1968 revealed the power of the play instinct in creating political awareness, although the lack of theoretical basis limited its ability to change things. We ought to celebrate freedom more, as in a festival. Such, at any rate, is Francis Hearn's theoretical analysis, although it seems to me that this implies a confusion between political and religious activity, since the phenomenon of the festival is far more religious than political, because of its transgressive nature.

Marcuse also referred to "the gigantic socialist utopia of Fourier" when criticizing Marx and Engels. He stated, "As Marx and Engels themselves acknowleged, Fourier was the only one to have made clear this qualitative difference between free and unfree society."[100] He explained that it is not necessary to opt for scientific rather than utopian socialism. Instead, the most revolutionary elements of each should be sought. As mentioned earlier, Marcuse believed that the path to socialism might move from science to utopia and not from utopia to science.[101] But in the final analysis, it is the utopian notion of socialism that really contains the innovative idea or *idée neuve*, as Marcuse put it.[102] This criticism of Marxism was so penetrating that in Jean-Michel Besnier's words, Fourier "constitutes an argument to dereify our revolutionary hopes, paralyzed by Marxism."[103]

Marcuse's references to Fourier were generally brief. Nevertheless, the latter was enormously important to his critical theory, since it was from Fourier that Marcuse took the idea of "qualitative difference" that alone makes it possible to redefine socialism in an affluent society. Marx defined socialism in relation to a poor society, whereas Marcuse felt we must redefine it in relation to the affluent society that has now developed.[104] For the first time in history, we are called upon to free ourselves from a society that functions relatively well and is relatively rich. In order for the transition from capitalism to socialism to equate liberation from the affluent society, we must stop defining socialism as the planned development of the means of production and the rationalization of resources. Obviously, such rationalization remains a precondition of all liberation. But we must redefine the characteristics of socialist society, particularly its "qualitative difference" from all established societies. For, wrote Marcuse, "if this qualitative difference today appears as Utopian, as idealistic, as metaphysical, this is precisely the form in which these radical features must appear if they are really to be a *definite negation* of the established society."[105] What, we may ask, are the characteristics of future socialist society? Presupposing a new anthropology and a total change in values, they are: the abolition of labor, the termination of the struggle for existence or the "pacification of existence," and the liberation of a new sensitivity or a new consciousness.[106] How are we to achieve this? From the negative standpoint, Marcuse explained, it would not be a question of revolution but of qualitative change: "I say intentionally 'of qualitative change,' not 'of revolution,' because we know of too many revolutions through which the continuum of repression has been sustained, revolutions which have replaced one system of domination by another."[107] On the positive side, he listed the convergence of technology with art, of work with play, and of the realm of necessity with the realm of freedom. This is what Fourier's "qualitative difference" has become in Marcuse's terms. It is the most radical, most utopian possibility of liberation today, an "aesthetic reality—society as a work of art."[108]

Before moving on, I want to discuss a further question in relation to Fourier—one that Marcuse appeared to ignore. What has happened to the utopian image of the polyvalent man that Marx and Engels borrowed from Fourier's description of "attractive labor"? Fourier's vision of future life showed man working with a variety of groups—hunters, farmers, fishermen, and so on—then going to a library, or "to museums, balls, the theater, and receptions."[109] This image of the polyvalent man reappears in *The German Ideology*: "In a communist society, where nobody has one exclusive sphere of activity but each can become accomplished in any branch he wishes, society regulates the general production and thus makes it possible for me to do one thing today and another tomorrow, to hunt in the morning, fish in the afternoon, rear cattle in the evening, criticize after dinner, just as I have a mind, without ever becoming hunter, fisherman, shepherd or critic."[110] Marcuse attributed Fourier's image to Marx, and seemed concerned with its significance. In 1965, he wrote that it contained "an unfortunate kernel of truth."[111] By 1966 he saw the image as a "monstrosity,"[112] and in 1969 rejected it as no longer "applicable to a highly developed industrial society."[113]

We have been looking at influences on Marcuse's thought in the realm of pure imagination. What about his frame of reference with regard to pure action, as exemplified by Mikhail

Bakunin? For Marcuse, the two were not mutually exclusive, but mutually inclusive. This seems to be the implication of his reply to Raymond Polin at the major international colloquium in Paris organized by UNESCO to commemorate the 150th anniversary of Karl Marx's birth. Significantly, the colloquium coincided with the first few days of the May 1968 student rebellion. Marcuse presented a paper entitled "Re-examination of the Concept of Revolution,"[114] which stimulated the following exchange:

> Question: Do you predict a recurrence of nihilism? Do you want to revive Bakunin and Kropotkin? Are you an anarchist?
>
> Answer: Am I an anarchist? No, although I feel no antipathy toward Kropotkin and Bakunin. *But if I had to acknowledge a master, it would more likely be Fourier.*"[115]

In order to avoid the accusation of being an anarchist, Marcuse turned to Fourier. He did not reject anarchism, however. For him, "the anarchic element is an essential factor in the struggle against domination,"[116] and radical revolt includes "a strong element of spontaneity, even anarchism."[117] He even considered it the role of the New Left to direct "spontaneous protest into organized action," and the "transformation of immediate into organized spontaneity."[118] What he hoped to see come about through some form of utopian action was a disciplined anarchism on the lines of Fourier's phalansterian community. An interesting comparison can be drawn between this assertion and a statement made in 1971 before sixteen hundred people at the University of California. Marcuse stated: "Anarchism should be incorporated into Marxism, but to do it now, in the face of powerful external enemies, is premature. . . . Today, it is a question of organization and cooperation."[119] He therefore made a distinction between his own thought and that of "the Movement." In his 1968 remarks he spoke for himself, whereas in 1971 he expressed what the New Left *should be* now, compared to what it *is*. In other words, he saw it as being infected with an anti-intellectualism that was damaging "the Movement" and the university. Furthermore, as he pointed out, "You don't cut off the branch on which you are sitting," and it was therefore necessary to take "one step backward in order to take two steps forward."[120] This step backward, which was very important to him, represented the entire utopian tradition, including anarchism. Notwithstanding the statement of François Perroux, for whom Marcuse did "not seem inclined toward an anarchic utopia,"[121] the evidence obliges us to admit the contrary. In 1969, this eminent French economist introduced him to the Collège de France as "the best analyst," whose "teaching was essential," possibly because he expressed himself "in terms clear enough to be scrawled on walls," even if they were "summary and illiterate."[122] In the same year Marcuse stated in *An Essay on Liberation* that "the anarchic element is an essential factor in the struggle against domination."[123]

Marcuse's anarchism was similar to Bakunin's in at least three major respects: the interpretation of negativity, the choice of "revolutionary subject," and the notion of revolutionary art. Bakunin's philosophic studies brought him into the Hegelian Left movement. According to Henri Arvon, he was especially taken with "the Hegelian notion of negativity, which he interpreted as the absolute need for humanity to promote its future through the total destruction of the status quo."[124] For Marcuse, by way of comparison, "Marxian theory . . . can no longer unfold the dialectic as logic,"[125] unless it makes it "a logic of *liberation*,"[126] a language that "breaks the power of facts"[127] because "the whole is false."[128]

As can be seen, the negativity theories of Marcuse and Bakunin were very close. The most striking resemblance, however, concerned the choice of "revolutionary subject." Comparison has seldom been made, but Arthur Mitchell in *The Major Works of Herbert Marcuse* and Gil Green in *The New Radicalism: Anarchist or Marxist?* have done so.[129] We need only look at the following three extracts, the first two from *One-Dimensional Man*, the third from Bakunin, to appreciate the justice of such comparison.

> Underneath the conservative popular base is the substratum of the outcasts and outsiders, the exploited and persecuted of other races and other colors, the unemployed and the unemployable.[130]

> . . . those who form the human base of the social pyramid—the outsiders and the poor, the unemployed and unemployable, the persecuted colored races, the inmates of prisons and mental institutions.[131]

> By the flower of the proletariat I mean exactly that eternal, basic material of government, that Great Unwashed which, being almost totally untouched by bourgeois civilization, carries within it the seed of future socialism—in its passions, instincts, aspirations, in all the needs and miseries of its collective situation. It alone is powerful enough to initiate and achieve the Social Revolution.[132]

How can one seriously profess Marxism while praising the *Lumpenproletariat* so often denigrated by Marx and Engels, unless one adopts Marx's own dictum: "I am not a Marxist"? Engels, for example, thought that anyone "invoking this absolutely venal and impudent rabble" was "a traitor to the cause."[133] Incidentally, Bakunin was Marx's principle adversary in the First International. Marcuse was similarly "a traitor to the cause," a self-styled "fink," as mentioned earlier.[134] Bakunin and Marcuse seemed to share some fundamental, physiological need for revolutionary activity transcending this or that anticapitalist group. The Bakunin extract above reveals this. Marcuse, in *An Essay on Liberation*, considered it a genuine instinct.

There is, I feel, one last point of similarity between Bakunin and Marcuse, and this is their conception of revolutionary art. Although "Bakunin did not devote any specific work to art," as André Reszler pointed out,[135] he nevertheless saw a truly revolutionary potential in the eternal "great art" of the past. I will not enlarge on Reszler's excellent study here, although later I will be discussing the role assigned by Marcuse to art in revolution.

Whether Marcuse went further than Bakunin is an interesting question. The latter's mission, according to his *Confession*, was to destroy, not build.[136] Marcuse felt we must first demolish our prison, even if we have no detailed blueprint for the house that will replace it.[137] Both felt we could put off building a new society until some later date. The task at hand was to prepare the way for the revolution.

The word "revolution" has an almost mesmerizing effect on intellectuals. A victim of the Stalin regime said that it was endowed with such an impressive force that it was impossible to understand why the prisons and mass executions were necessary. The power of the word was almost enough in itself to sap intellectual opposition.[138] This testimony supports Jules Monnerot's statement at the beginning of *Sociologie et révolution*, to the effect that "the word 'revolution' is always taken in *good* part. When it ceases to be understood thus, we will have moved into a new era."[139] Jacques Ellul felt that this was already happening: "I think that Western society is actually entering an era of meaningless revolution,"[140] and Raymond Aron entitled his analysis of the May 1968 student protest *La Révolution introuvable*—literally "the unfindable revolution."[141] As François Châtelet pointed out, the history of the concept of revolution reveals its two sides: revolution based on an established model, as in Plato and St. Augustine; and revolution without a model, which takes shape in relation to a model yet to be constructed, or one in the process of being created, as in Pericles, Machiavelli, Lenin, and Mao Tse-tung.[142] The latter side, according to Gilles Lapouge, could be defined as utopian,[143] and it was to this utopian tradition of revolution, without model or meaning, that Marcuse adhered. The irony is that in the final analysis Marcuse, the convinced revolutionary intellectual, persuaded no one of the need for revolution. Why?

Habermas asked Marcuse in an interview how a model for revolutionary change could be conceived today. Marcuse replied, "The revolution itself will be an entirely different project than it was for Marx," because "we have to look for a model for revision according to which revolution will occur not because of progressive economic deterioration, etc., but rather on the existing basis of the so-called consumer society."[144] In his analysis of Bahro's work, he was even more categorical. "Today it is evident to what degree the Marxist-Leninist model for revolution has become historically obsolete. . . . Is it possible to develop another model of revolution on the basis of the current tendencies in class relations?"[145] The fact is that revolutionary masses have no chance of succeeding in an armed uprising, because the military organization of the dominant class is too powerful. Furthermore, these same masses have become integrated into the social structure. For both these reasons, argued Marcuse, if we are to construct another revolutionary model by reexamining Marxism, we need an Ariadne's thread to guide us through the labyrinth. Because of the enormous stabilizing potential of today's society, any Marxist analysis of the period of transition to total socialism must take into account a form of socialism "*that does not yet actually exist*," so that "the concrete utopia . . . becomes the guiding thread of the empirical analysis," with the end or "transcendence" of utopia appearing as a necessity.[146]

What is meant by the necessity of revolution? Donald Lee has given us a very detailed study of the concept of necessity. Lee was Marcuse's student and later teaching assistant for a course in social and political philosophy, and subsequently taught the same subject from the Marcusian standpoint. He came "to the disappointing conclusion that Marcuse was after all *wrong* in his interpretation of what Marx *meant*, but fruitful in his reinterpretation (revision?) of Marx."[147]

Lee acknowledged that Marx had often been criticized for having affirmed the necessity or inevitability of the socialist victory. He cited numerous sources in support of Marcuse's contention that, in Marx's later work, this meaning of necessity entails the negative development of capitalism, but not the positive transformation toward socialism. The whole of Marx's message could only be understood if one took into account his early works, where he demonstrated the positive content of the necessity, *in the sense of a moral duty*, for development of a more rational and humane society. Marcuse therefore rejected Marx's notion of scientific historic determinism, while linking himself to the ethic of the socialist tradition by visualizing utopia and revolution as two dimensions of the same need. As Maximilien Rudel explained, "Utopia is the dimension of space, and revolution the dimension of time."[148]

The socialist movement considers itself as both utopian and revolutionary. Utopia is the *telos* that guides the militant toward the creation of a new state; revolution is the will to abolish existing forms of society. Revolution and utopia therefore combine to create the normative foundations of socialist ethics. Revolutionary spirit and utopian faith meet in ethical necessity. It is therefore not surprising that Marcuse's principle work on revolution should be entitled *Ethics and Revolution*.[149]

Marcuse admitted that he had always been a revolutionary.[150] Yet in 1932 he had used the word *reform* to describe political and economic revolution. He rejected it in favor of a demand for *total revolution*.[151] The main revolutionary problem was not socialization of the means of production, as this could not resolve the question of liberty and repression. In 1941 he gave the title *Reason and Revolution* to his second attempt at interpreting Hegel's philosophy, but nowhere did he analyze or explain the concept of revolution, as Guinle remarked in his review.[152] Why was this? Probably, as his 1967 article on "The Obsolescence of Marxism" revealed, it was because "Marx's own idea of socialism was . . . not utopian enough."[153] However, according to an interview filmed the same year on "Liberation From the Affluent Society," Marcuse also considered that past revolutions had perpetuated repression, and therefore only qualitative change, not revolution, could produce a new man.[154] The only definition of revolution which we appear to have is in *Ethics and Revolution*. Marcuse wrote, "Let me define what I mean by 'revolution.' By 'revolution' I understand the overthrow of a legally established government and constitution by a social class or movement with the aim of altering the social as well as the political structure. This definition excludes all military coups, palace revolutions, and 'preventive' counter-revolutions (such as Fascism and Nazism) because they do not alter the basic social structure."[155] This definition first appeared in the original German edition of 1965. In May 1968, during the UNESCO symposium on *Marx and Contemporary Scientific Thought*, Marcuse gave a brief summary of the Marxist thesis, then offered some thoughts that were merely intended as guidelines for establishing a definition of a new concept.[156]

What was new about Marcuse's revolutionary theory in relation to Marx? A detailed comparative analysis of the two was attempted by Antony Ruprecht,[157] who sought to answer four questions that Marx and Engels posed in *The German Ideology*.[158]

To begin with, under what conditions can a revolution take place? Marx felt that, in accordance with the scientific laws of dialectical materialism, the internal contradictions of the capitalist system (by which he meant the inherent antagonism between the means and the relations of production) would explode in revolution, as happened during the transition from slavery to feudalism, and from feudalism to capitalism.[159] Marcuse, on the contrary, considered that the dialectical movement of history had been neutralized by the assimilating tendencies of the capitalist system.[160]

What, therefore, are the conditions that engender revolutionary consciousness? For Marx, revolutionary consciousness was determined by material conditions.[161] Once he became aware of his alienation from his work, the worker would be ready to develop a revolutionary consciousness.[162] For Marcuse, however, revolutionary consciousness required "political education," because the worker could not develop it by himself.[163] While is true that Marx wrote *The Communist Manifesto* to educate the proletariat and develop its revolutionary consciousness, such education was considered an auxiliary function. With Marcuse, it became the essential task.[164]

After the development of revolutionary consciousness in response to the material conditions of society came the question of who should carry out the revolution. We know that Marx attributed the role of revolutionary agent to the proletariat.[165] As Julien Freund remarked, "It was a brilliant idea to lump the bourgeois of the world into a single group, and the proletariat of the world into another, these groups being revolutionary opposites. It injected new vigor into political life at a moment when the dominant doctrines were trying to neutralize politics. We need look no further to find the reasons for Marxism's success."[166] However, in *One-Dimensional Man*, Marcuse asserted that "the reality of the laboring classes in advanced industrial society makes the Marxian 'proletariat' a mythological concept."[167] In one of his last lectures he again set forth the concept of the reification of the proletariat.[168] He was in fact saying that capitalist society had succeeded in transforming personal relationships between workers into objective relationships between things, a process of reification that he had already expounded in *Reason and Revolution*.[169] Marcuse did not therefore rely on one class of workers or the proletariat as a group sufficiently outside the system to attack it. He looked, rather, toward a group capable of providing future guidance in all cultural sectors. Marcuse, explained Richard King, removed the problem of revolutionary thought from the political to the cultural arena.[170] He expected more from a change of consciousness than from the overthrow of external structures. Although he agreed that the revolution could only be brought about by "the majority of the population,"[171] he was looking for the activist minority that would light the fuse of the insurrectionist movement. He had no desire to stage an armed march on the Capitol, in the style of Blanqui, nor was he attracted by Lenin's method, whereby the party controlled the masses. His position was closer to that of Cohn-Bendit and the tradition of Rosa Luxemburg, for whom, as Jean-Paul Sartre explained, it was the leaders emerging from the masses at each stage who would spark the insurrectional movement—leaders who would appear, play their part, and disappear.[172] "The search for specific historical agents of revolutionary change in the advanced capitalist countries is indeed meaningless. *Revolutionary forces emerge in the process of change itself*; the translation of the potential into the actual is the work of political practice."[173]

If we abandon class-based Marxism, where can we find the revolutionary subject? Harvey Wheeler put this question to Marcuse, who replied: "I have been bothered about this for a long time, and I'm afraid I cannot give you a satisfactory answer. The only thing I can say is that it seems to me wrong to go around looking for agents of historical change. They probably will arise and become identifiable only during the process of change itself."[174]

Even so, Marcuse still attempted to define the revolutionary subject. During a congress at Korčula, for example, he stated: "It is that class or group which, by virtue of its function and position in society, is in vital need and is capable of risking what they have and what they can get within the established system in order to replace this system—a radical change which would indeed involve destruction, abolition of the existing system."[175] He went on to explain that such a group should at least be capable of utilizing its vital need for revolution, if not to trigger it, at least to end it. To the extent that we employ the Marxist notion of "revolutionary subject, we have to say that revolution without the industrial working class is still unimaginable,"[176] even though most workers in advanced industrial societies have no such vital need. But, asked Marcuse, can one reconcile these two obviously conflicting realities? In his answer, he referred to the Marxist tradition and the distinction between the revolutionary subject *an sich*, and the revolutionary subject *für sich*. He thus showed that the working class is still the revolutionary subject in itself, but not for itself, because it is not only *in* the capitalist system but also *of* the system.[177] But what, he then asked, are the chances of increasing its revolutionary potential? This class must react against its integration at all costs, by becoming conscious of the intolerable conditions in which it lives. It is not only the misery and poverty that are intolerable, but the agressivity, waste, brutality, and hypocrisy of our society, not to mention the many ways in which it perpetuates the old forms of the struggle for existence through poverty, exploitation, and all manner of inhuman working conditions. This is why the task of developing a radical political consciousness falls to groups that are not integrated into the system of domination, to groups who want to develop a radical conscience because they are aware of the vital need for revolution, not only with regard to institutions or labor relations, but also with regard to the revolutionary subject itself: the type of man, his values, and his aspirations.

In "The Obsolescence of Marxism,"[178] Marcuse distinguished four possible elements of the "syndrome of revolutionary potential." These consisted of national liberation movements in underdeveloped countries; workers' movements based on a "new strategy" combining traditional Marxism and syndicalism; the lowest orders of the welfare state; and the opposition of the intelligentsia.[179] He emphasized, however, that there was little point trying to raise the level of a consciousness that was well-nigh imperceptible; it was rather a question of trying to create one in the first place.[180] Why was he so pessimistic? Three years earlier, in "Socialism in Developed Countries," a paper delivered at the aforementioned Korčula, he concluded with the remarks: "This would not be the first time in history that the real historic subject of the revolution could not be identified. There have been times in the past when the historic subject was latent. This does not invalidate Marxism. The concepts which Marx originated should not be rejected but developed; their further development is already contained in the basic thesis. This is why we can and must permit pessimism, in its proper place."[181]

Let us come back to the fourth point of comparison between the revolutionary theory of Marx and Marcuse. It concerns the inevitability of the transformation of capitalism into socialism. According to Marx and Engels, the socialist revolution is necessary and inevitable. The advance of socialism is governed by inexorable dialectical laws. Revolution makes it possible to sweep away "all the muck" of the old system and "found society anew."[182] But Marcuse, in his determination to root his own critical theory in the Hegelian-Marxist tradition in *Reason and Revolution*, left aside the determinist approach in favor of only the volontarist point of view: "The revolution requires the maturity of many forces, but the greatest among them is the subjective force, namely, the revolutionary class itself."[183] In other words, it is the revolutionaries themselves who carry forward the whole future of humanity by their ethical choice and the justification they give to the revolutionary cause.[184] However, they must first rid themselves of Marxist positivist prejudice, which engenders a belief in the necessary and inexorable nature of a transition toward some higher stage of human evolution, and in the success of this transition.[185] Lastly, the revolutionaries are morally bound to justify the use of revolutionary violence. In "The Problem of Violence and the Radical Opposition," Marcuse explained that: "The concept of violence covers two different forms: the institutionalized violence of the established system and the violence of resistance, which is necessarily illegal in relation to positive law. It is meaningless to speak of the legality of resistance: no social sytem, even the freest, can constitutionally legalize violence directed against itself. Each of these forms has functions that conflict with those of the other. There is violence of suppression and violence of liberation; there is violence for the defense of life and violence of aggression."[186]

Violence has always existed. Our societies are by nature given to conflict. History is littered with wars and revolts of all kinds. In the past such unhappy circumstances were considered a misfortune. But Marcuse, in keeping with the most radical doctrines, justified recourse to violence in advance. Does the end therefore justify the means? When questioned by Louis Wiznitzer on this point, he replied that the end did not justify the means when the "forces of order" intervened in Nigeria, Indonesia, or Vietnam.[187] But in "Ethics and Revolution" he wrote: "Can the revolutionary justify *all* means? . . . In one sense, the end justifies the means, namely, if they demonstrably serve human progress in freedom."[188] On the basis of reason, he therefore claimed to legitimize a need for change that would be vital in terms of eschatological and utopian ends, such as total liberation of the human species. In practice, the better the cause, the less justification needed; with Marcuse's theory, on the contrary, justification is apparently bound to increase, because the realization of concrete objectives undermines the cause. I mentioned earlier that, not satisfied with calling himself "a fink,"[189] he added to his arsenal of justifications the comment, "You don't cut off the branch on which you are sitting."[190] Nevertheless, it seems to me that the revolution is nothing if it does not remove at least some of the branch. In the event, Marcuse covered himself by calling on a particular group of specialists to spearhead revolution. On one hand, in "The End of Utopia" he took a pessimistic view of "the class of technicians, scientists, etc." who are "precisely . . . among the highest paid and rewarded beneficiaries of the system." The likelihood of their becoming a potential revolutionary force "would require a total change not only of consciousness but of the whole situation"—or, as Marcuse expressed it in the preface to the French edition of *One-Dimensional Man,* "a miracle of discernment and lucidity."[191] The optimistic view was that, on the other hand, "intellectuals have the major duty of seeing that the specialists of the future . . . become *specialists in liberation,*" or "specialists of peace."[192]

In the final analysis, pessimism and optimism were intertwined to the point of becoming a way of thinking, a mode or mentality: utopia became utopianism, and the revolution, revolutionarism. Discourse had to be all the more revolutionary for not being translated into action. But was this not totally opposed to Marx's position? Frederic Jameson asserted that this was indeed the case. For him, Marcuse's theory represented a form of Marxist interpretation designed to show that the task of philosophy is to regenerate the utopian thrust. In the words of *Eros and Civilization*, it should outline "a theoretical construct of culture beyond the performance principle,"[193] with the result that the Marcusian perspective is the inverse of the Marxist. With Marx, utopia dissipates revolutionary energy, whereas with Marcuse, it is practical thought that dissipates revolutionary energy, because historical conditions are no longer the same. In the earlier society described by Marx, utopian thought was directed toward the accomplishment of imaginary desires, and thus dissipated revolutionary energy. In today's society, what obstructs revolutionary energy is the practical outlook that gives in to the system, because it sees that the system is able to integrate everything, even its adversaries. In our advanced industrial society, only utopia can take the form of a determinate negation of the status quo, keep alive the possibility of a qualitatively different world, and revive revolutionary energy. In a 1974 lecture given in Frankfurt on "Theory and Practice"[194] Marcuse emphasized the "kernel of idealism" that historical materialism "contained from the beginning." This kernel was the presence of utopia at the heart of revolutionary action, "a utopia without which Marxist theory cannot serve as a guide to socialist practice." Such a utopia appears today "as a project" to be born in the "emancipated conscience that will determine the social being" after the "qualitative leap," that is to say, when conditions are ripe for "an economy aimed at the elimination of poverty and exploitation." But the project is blocked. Essentially, Marcuse's most famous works are a description of economic, psychological, and other types of obstruction. However, even if we are today facing an "impossible revolution," the historical possibility of realizing utopia should give us moral support.

We could, at this juncture, be tempted to agree with the fairly current interpretation which says that the vacuum of the Marxist utopia is filled by Marcuse's Freudian conception of man. But to slip into Freudo-Marxism would merely add to the intense "mythification" that took place after the Paris rebellion of May 1968, as Gerhard Höhn and Gérard Raulet pointed out.[195] French commentators have not yet really absorbed the critical contribution of the Frankfurt School, either ignoring or rejecting it out of hand.[196] There are, in fact, several very specific points that must be understood in order to grasp Marcusian utopian theory. Of the many elements neglected by French scholars, I have chosen those with which they seem least familiar. To understand the historical period in question, let us first look at this passage by Martin Jay:

> The Frankfurt School was returning to the concerns of the Left Hegelians of the 1840s. Like that first generation of critical theorists, its members were interested in the integration of philosophy and social analysis. They likewise were concerned with the dialectical method devised by Hegel and sought, like their predecessors, to turn it in a materialist direction. And finally, like many of the Left Hegelians, they were particularly interested in exploring the possibilities of transforming the social order through human *praxis*.
>
> The intervening century, however, had brought enormous changes, which made the conditions of their theorizing vastly different. Whereas the Left Hegelians were the immediate successors of the classical German idealists, the Frankfurt School was separated from Kant and Hegel by Schopenhauer, Nietzsche, Dilthey, Bergson,

> Weber, Husserl, and many others, not to mention the systematization of Marxism itself. As a result, Critical Theory had to reassert itself against a score of competitors who had driven Hegel from the field. And, of course, it could not avoid being influenced by certain of their ideas.[197]

It is my contention that, among all these opposing doctrines, there were two that had a marked influence on Marcuse and that have too often been ignored by his critics. We must make a special place in Marcuse's background for Rosa Luxemburg and Karl Mannheim.

There are two reasons for emphasizing the relationship between Luxemburg and Marcuse. The first is that Marcuse's revolutionary spirit was linked, by his own admission, to that of Rosa Luxemburg. Secondly, it was Luxemburg who originated the slogan, "socialism or barbarism."

Rosa Luxemburg was a figurehead of Weimar culture to which Marcuse belonged. It has been described by Walter Laqueur, professor of history at Tel Aviv, as "the first authentically modern culture."[198] Luxemburg belonged to an era of such upheaval that Alfred Kantorowicz wrote, "The radicalist tendency is quite understandable; all the roots of subsequent turmoil date from this era."[199] As a militant revolutionary within the German Social Democratic party, Luxemburg denounced reformism. Some of her articles were collected in 1899 in the German edition of *Social Reform or Revolution*.[200] She explained what she meant by this alternative in a short preface.[201] Marcuse used the same terms during discussion with students of the West Berlin Free University following his paper on "The Problem of Violence and the Radical Opposition."[202] They weren't advocating opposition to reform within the established order. In one sense, all revolutionaries work within this order. The idea was never to lose sight of the final objective, the revolution that will abolish the capitalist regime. The final objective, wrote Rosa Luxemburg, is the only decisive element that distinguishes the socialist movement from bourgeois democracy and bourgeois radicalism.[203]

As for the slogan, "socialism or barbarism,"[204] Marcuse considered it more appropriate than ever.[205] He saw it as an intregral part of the concept of revolution,[206] representing a historic choice for the Subject: "The Subject is free to choose:

in this choice of a possible historical *praxis* which transcends the established praxis is the essence of human freedom. And this freedom is not a 'fact', neither a transcendental nor a historical fact—it is the faculty (and activity) of men 'synthesizing' (organizing) the data of experience so that they reveal their own (objective) negativity, namely, the degree to which they are the data of domination."[207] How does this dilemma arise, and what does it mean? Michael Loewy wrote a chapter on "The Methodological Meaning of the Slogan 'Socialism or Barbarism.' "[208] On the basis of Lukács's arguments, he explained that before 1914 German social democracy asked whether socialism was the inevitable product of economic and historic development, or the result of a moral option inspired by pure intentions.[209] Dialectically speaking, however, Rosa Luxemburg transcended this question in the formula "socialism or barbarism." Toward the end of the *Junius* pamphlet,[210] she referred to a passage in Engels' *Anti-Dühring*.[211] Michael Loewy, however, was of the view that, "in the final analysis, it was *Rosa Luxemburg herself* who (while basing herself on Engels) *explicitly* posited socialism as being, not the 'inevitable' product of historical necessity, but an objective historical *possibility*. In this sense, the slogan 'socialism or barbarism' means that, in history, *the options are always open*: the 'final victory' or defeat of the proletariat has not been decided in advance by the 'ironclad laws' of economic determinism; it also depends on the conscious action and revolutionary will of this proletariat."[212] "Socialism or barbarism" therefore means that there is not *only one* direction in which to develop, but *several*, and that a decision must consequently be made as to the best historical process. In Marcuse's work, however, this meaning was limited to the use of this "classic alternative" in the singular, so as to show that once again fascism was threatening to bar the route to socialism.[213] This is why we must "develop consciousness to provoke a revolutionary situation—without losing sight of the fact that the latter can just as well herald the advent of a new fascism."[214] Both Rosa Luxemburg and Marcuse felt that the options were open, however, and that the task of preparation was as formidable as the objective—the ultimate goal. This is why utopia appeared indispensable. As a twentieth century philosopher, however, Marcuse could not ignore Karl Mannheim, even in the context of utopia as part of a revolutionary platform. He understood the significance of Mannheim, and was to some extent influenced by him.

The mere mention of the name Mannheim is enough to arouse controversy. Rejected by some, respected by others, he certainly cannot be ignored, as Edward Shils demonstrated in 1973.[215] According to Jean-Michel Palmier, "Any attempt to revive utopia in modern political thinking must first deal with the critique of Karl Mannheim, expounded in the now classic work, *Ideology and Utopia* (1929)."[216] On the other hand if we were guided by Raymond Ruyer, for whom "Mansheim's [*sic*] distinctions between ideology and utopia seem fairly artificial and of little interest,"[217] we could dismiss Mannheim in three sentences, as Ruyer did in his work on *L'Utopie et les utopies*.[218] (Incidentally, "*Mansh*eim" is a marvellous *lapsus calami*, as *mansh* means mishmash or jumble in German.) Between the two extremes of Palmier and Ruyer, it seems to me there is room for a more moderate judgment. Joseph Gabel, for example, defended a *doctorat ès lettres* thesis at the Sorbonne in 1962 on the subject of "Mannheim and Hungarian Marxism." In his revised version, he stated that certain aspects of Mannheim's thought "presage what is best in Herbert Marcuse."[219]

We can see an example of this in the historical role of the *Freischwebende Intelligenz*, which Lucien Goldmann translated as *intellectualité sans attaches* (intellectuality without strings)[220] and Gabel suggested translating as "marginal intelligentsia."[221] Gabel made it clear that in Weimar Germany the universities had an enviable social status which was not without strings, and that Mannheim was not thinking of his colleagues when he developed his theory of marginal intelligentsia. We do not need to speculate on Marcuse's opinion of this subject, since Goldmann, "one of Mannheim's principal French opponents"[222] put the question to him during a debate at the Ecole pratique des hautes études. Is there an objective social force capable of transcending contradictions and controlling history? In other words, given the fact, as both Mannheim and the Marxists admitted, that the scholar belongs to a given class or social group and reflects its outlook, can he possibly rise above it? And given the variety of social groups and points of view, is it possible to "synthesize perspectives"? And *who* will carry out this synthesis? Here is Marcuse's answer: "For Hegel, there is only one privilege (and I agree with Hegel on this point): the privilege of thought, the primacy of thought. In the open arena of history, under the reign of freedom, thought would be universal, and all men would have access to this privileged status. We must know the world before changing it. Hence the primacy of science and knowledge in guiding social and political action."[223] Marcuse was therefore emphasizing the role of intellectuals. However, he took marginal thinkers into account as well, as we saw when discussing Bakunin. Furthermore, Marcuse extended this privileged role to the people, the majority, and "all men." He was not interested in knowing what single group—proletariat or otherwise—would have a privileged role. He was looking at the greatest possible number of groups in seeking the will for change, a will that the proletariat had lost because "the reality of the laboring classes in advanced industrial society makes the Marxian 'proletariat' a mythological concept."[224] As for Mannheim, he considered Marxism a proletarian ideology every bit as partisan as the ideologies of other classes.[225]

How, then, could Marcuse, who with his Frankfurt Institute colleagues desired to defend Marxism, look with favor on the work of Mannheim, who saw Marxism as merely one ideology among many? We can understand this paradox better in the light of the circumstances surrounding the original publication of *Ideology and Utopia* in 1929. Mannheim's work stemmed from a controversy between Bloch and Lukács on utopia.[226] At the time, Mannheim was a professor at the University of Frankfurt-am-Main.[227] Occasionally he even worked on the institute premises.[228] His work, explained Paul Breines, was in the nature of a challenge to the interpretations of Marxism put forward by Lukács in *History and Class Consciousness* and Korsch in *Marxism and Philosophy*, both of which first appeared in 1923.[229]

Mannheim sought to destroy Marxism's claim to having a prerogative on historical truth. He took some of the Marxist theories and incorporated them into a bourgeois sociology for the purpose of refuting Marxism in its entirety.

Marcuse reviewed Mannheim's work in the same year as it came out.[230] What strikes the reader most, wrote Martin Jay, is how favorably Marcuse reacted,[231] even though "Mannheim seemed to be undermining the basic Marxist distinction between true and false consciousness."[232] According to Mannheim, "the common and, in the last analysis, essential element of the concepts of ideology and utopia is that both imply the possibility of false consciousness."[233] For Marcuse, however, "When critical theory comes to terms with philosophy, it is interested in the truth content of philosophical concepts and problems. It presupposes that they really contain truth. The enterprise of the sociology of knowledge, to the contrary, is occupied only with the untruths, not the truths of previous philosophy."[234] What Marcuse finally reproached Mannheim for was his interpretation of historical being.[235] The concept of historical being has possibilities that are at present blocked by organized capitalism, explained James Schmidt. These should be evaluated to see whether there is a chance of realizing them through revolution.[236] But what Marcuse clearly appreciated in Mannheim was that, for him, utopia retained all its creative value. As Roger Bastide pointed out, Mannheim considered that all ideas were utopian which transcended the status quo (and were not merely the projection of our desires), and that had to some degree the power to change the historical and social order.[237] Still, it must not be forgotten that their interpretions of the end of utopia were diametrically opposed. Marcuse, in "The End of Utopia," spoke of the possible achievement of utopia thanks to technology. But Mannheim evoked the decline of utopia as a result of scientific thinking and "the concept of historical time which led to qualitatively different epochs."[238]

All in all, was there any great affinity between Mannheim and Marcuse? I have been referring to the commentaries of Martin Jay and James Schmidt, among others, although I might also have cited the interesting study by Joseph Devitis.[239] The most eloquent testimony, however, and one that seems unknown to commentators, is by one of Marcuse's students, David Kettler, who reported the lectures given at Columbia University when the State Department invited Marcuse to talk about Marxism in 1951.[240] Marcuse concentrated on the breakdown of "critical rationalism" at the end of the Roman era. He pointed out that this basic philosophical tradition can turn into an ideology, in such a way that social protest against repressive conditions can only take the form of utopia, doomed to remain powerless. The process can take one of the three following forms. Ideas are given a place in a sphere that totally transcends man's concrete conditions, so that it is impossible to reply to these ideas except through the intermediary of utopian novels or visionary tales. Again, ideas may be internalized so that their realization becomes a matter of internal reorganization; in this case, one cannot preach change except on the basis of an imaginary conception of revolution handed down from on high. Finally, the vision contained in these ideas may be reserved for an elite, thus leaving no means of protest for the rest, except pathetic and foredoomed slave uprisings. This Marcusian typology of ideology and utopia echoes much that is in Mannheim, and indeed Mannheim's influence on Marcuse was more than superficial.

As we have seen, Marcuse shaped his vision of utopia in the light of the work of distinguished and innovative predecessors. His exact place in this long heritage may be disputed, but there is no doubt of his imaginative contribution to the literature.

III

Marcuse's Romantic Aesthetics

"In a world that has descended to the prosaic, the most important thing to bring back is the aesthetic dimension . . . which alone can guarantee the revolution of the twenty-first century."[1] Marcuse was speaking about his short work, *The Aesthetic Dimension*, during a final conversation with Jean Marabini. "This is the heritage I leave to world youth on the threshold of the terrible years that seem imminent."[2]

It is no accident that Marcuse's philosophical testament should be a work on aesthetics. Throughout his life the question of art was central to Marcuse's thinking. His first academic dissertation in 1922 contained the seeds of several themes that were to mark his intellectual journey, and dealt with the German Künstlerroman, the genre of novel in which art plays a significant role.[3] It is therefore crucial to ask exactly what place the aesthetic dimension occupies in the critical theory of Herbert Marcuse.

Before we can answer this question, however, there is a preliminary problem to be resolved. The fact is that, while some commentators ignore or are unaware of Marcuse's explicit utopianism, others have read into Marcusian aesthetics mere resignation instead of the renewal of his revolutionary spirit. Ben Agger and Fred Alford were two cases in point. In 1973 Agger wrote an article entitled "The Aesthetic Politics of Herbert Marcuse." Referring to *Counterrevolution and Revolt*, Agger represented Marcuse's interest in art as the most recent development in his critical theory.[4] This was largely untrue. Not only was Marcuse always interested in art—it could be considered his main concern in one sense, as we shall see—but art was a symbol of the Great Refusal,[5] at least in its extreme forms. Agger contended that art does not take the place of politics, although it can "become political by maintaining a 'dialogue' with the natural world and with social fact." He pointed out that "Marcuse's argument is really quite simple and plausible: we create ourselves through our art which depicts our true relation to nature and to our fellow man and woman. Art raises our consciousness and helps us to imagine a new world. It acts as a theoretical and spiritual catalyst when all else has failed."[6] It is perhaps our only hope, Agger concluded. His interpretation was generally correct, except that he considered Marcuse's involvement in aesthetics as the final phase and ignored his early interest in the subject. This meant that six years later, in 1979, Agger would try to save Marcuse from "aesthetic resignation"[7] on the basis of Paul Piccone's notion of "artificial negativity."[8] Piccone asserted that it is possible to go beyond one-dimensionality by penetrating the world of spontaneous subjectivity. But surely spontaneity and creativity are both inherent aspects of art and the revolutionary spirit? (It should be mentioned in passing that Ben Agger is, in my view, one of the rare commentators who respects the spirit of Marcuse's work.)

Fred Alford also purported to save Marcuse from an impasse. In reviewing *The Aesthetic Dimension*,[9] he compared some of its statements with others taken from Marcuse's essay on Rudolf Bahro.[10] According to Alford, Marcuse's theory would have been trapped in a vicious circle, had he not been able to break out of it with Bahro's help. Alford wrote, "He did integrate Bahro's catalog into the structure of his own project, in order to begin to overcome its outstanding theoretical deficit: the vicious circle, which has led to so much unwarranted resignation. No assessment of Marcuse's work that fails to take seriously this last step can be complete."[11]

I shall refrain from commenting on the idea that Marcuse's theory can be better understood by referring to his sources instead of his own statements. A good many commentators have seen in Marcuse an interpretation of Marx, Freud, or some other writer—Bahro in this instance—whereas he almost never interpreted anyone, except in book reviews. Marcuse was a critical theorist who expressed his own ideas and whose thinking was not deflected by affinities of thought encountered in his long intellectual journey.

Alford found two basic tendencies in Marcuse: one good—his commitment to human happiness; the other bad—his romanticism. Fortunately, said Alford, Marcuse appeared to have sublimated the less desirable of these two tendencies in the following ways.[12] In the first place, Marcuse supposedly admitted in *The Aesthetic Dimension* that certain elements of his vision of liberation, such as "the resurrection of nature," would never be realized. Alford supported this by Marcuse's statement that "the world was not made for the sake of the human being and it has not become more human."[13] This freed Marcuse to solve the problem of "the vicious circle that recurs so often . . . in Bahro's book."[14] Alford wrote: "The way out of the vicious circle turns out to be remarkably easy. Bahro's book, says Marcuse, implies that socialist strategy must be essentially the same before and after the revolution. The cultural revolution implies the total transformation of society, but the subjects of the revolution must think and act today as they will after the revolution."[15] This, according to Alford, was the only means of avoiding aesthetic resignation and breaking out of the vicious circle. It was by no means the only way out, however; Marcuse stated his own view clearly in his essay on "Protosocialism and Late Capitalism." The only acceptable means of altering the status quo, he said, was through "Plato's position (an educational dictatorship of the most intelligent) and Rousseau's (people must be forced to be free)," and however scandalous it might seem, one had to uphold the paradox that a socialist state needs "a recognized . . . elite."[16]

But how did Marcusian aesthetics strive to renew the revolutionary spirit? To answer this question, we must establish Marcuse's objectivity in relation to Marxist aesthetics by defining and evaluating Marcusian aesthetics.

One of the errors of Marxist aesthetics, according to Marcuse, was "the denigration of romanticism as simply reactionary."[17] And yet romanticism, adventurism, or imagination form the basis of any revolution in Marcuse's view. "If the revolution does not contain an element of adventurism, it is worthless," he stated in a *L'Express* interview.[18] What did he mean by this romanticism, in this sense?

To begin with, even if the Romantic Movement *per se* was a nineteenth-century phenomenon, the elements were present in eighteenth-century culture. As Georges Gusdorf noted, "Not one of the elements of what was called Romanticism in the nineteenth century was absent from the arts and literature of the preceding century."[19] In "L'Existence esthétique," the last chapter of *Naissance de la conscience romantique au siècle des lumières*, Gusdorf demonstrated that the contemporary definition of aesthetic activity was fairly specific. He analyzed several essays on the arts, beginning with Baumgarten, who first used the word "aesthetic" in the manner specifically referred to by Marcuse in *Eros and Civilization*.[20] Consequently, there was no contradiction in Marcuse's attempt to trace aesthetic romanticism back through Marx to Fourier and beyond. The active cultivation of imaginative commitment and an emphasis on the creative will of the ego are rooted in a long tradition. In any case, even Marx contained romantic elements, and these were precisely what interested Marcuse.

The presence of these elements has not always been recognized. Michael Loewy, for example, in his 1976 sociological study on revolutionary intellectuals, wrote that "Marx's socialism has nothing to do with anticapitalist romanticism, sociologically or ideologically."[21] Fortunately, he later corrected this statement. Admitting the justice of criticism leveled by the Americans Paul Breines[22] and Jeffrey Herf,[23] he even went so far as to devote an entire book to the subject, *Marxisme et romantisme révolutionnaire*,[24] which included a demonstration of the profound influence of Thomas Carlyle[25] and Honoré de Balzac[26] on Marx and Engels. A year later, in a 1980 essay in *Telos*,[27] Loewy again emphasized the romantic dimension in the theory of Marcuse and Benjamin, although he weakened his argument somewhat by maintaining that there was a periodic waning of Marcuse's interest in aesthetic and romantic questions, and in the problem of art and culture.

If we look at the major stages in Marcuse's life outlined in chapter 1, it is evident that aesthetic and romantic considerations remained constant throughout his work. When completing his studies during the Weimar period, he produced "Der deutsche Künstlerroman," his 1922 dissertation on novels with the artist as protagonist. The central theme of this dissertation was "the contradiction between the world of Idea and empirical reality, art, and bourgeois life—a contradiction painfully perceived and expressed by the Romantics," as Loewy pointed out. Marcuse, he said, stressed "the burning aspiration of many Romantic or neo-Romantic writers for a radical change of life, bursting through the narrow limits of bourgeois philistine materialism," and compared them with "contemporary utopian socialists such as Fourier."[28] Loewy felt that Marcuse had repeated some of his earlier ideas without alteration in *Eros and Civilization* and *One-Dimensional Man*. Barry Katz explained that the issue raised in this dissertation reflected the neo-Hegelian principles of Georg Lukács outlined in *The Theory of the Novel* (1920). This work originally appeared in 1916, in a journal devoted to aesthetics and art criticism. The journal's director was Max Dessoir, one of Marcuse's teachers at the time. Consequently, Marcuse wrote very much in the style of a young romantic whose theory and method were taking root in the aesthetics of Hegel, "the most serious of all serious philosophers."[29]

During the period between 1933 and 1942, Marcuse's aesthetic interests centered on the Frankfurt School's analysis of mass culture. As Martin Jay noted,[30] he made a considerable contribution to this analysis. An example is his 1937 article, "The Affirmative Character of Culture." In the later phases of his work, beginning with *Eros and Civilization*, Marcuse's aesthetics and utopianism clearly assumed greater importance as his criticism became more radical. Marcuse's commentators generally ignore this fact, often more or less intentionally, depending on their view of Marxist orthodoxy. The more importance they attach to the latter, the less they give to the romanticism and libertarian idealism present in Marx himself.

Other scholars have readily admitted the importance of the romantic dimension in Marcuse's thought, either to criticize or commend it. Peter Clecak, for example, in an excellent 1973 study on Marcuse and the paradoxes of American radicalism, saw him as a romantic and revolutionary intellectual,[31] although this was apparently a reproach. In reviewing Clecak's study Richard Flacks concluded that the New Left need not shed its romanticism, and that adequate practical strategies would provide a balance.[32] The title of his article, "The Importance of the Romantic Myth for the Left," left no doubt on this score.

At the beginning of this chapter, I stated that Alford was wrong in believing that Marcuse could break out of the vicious circle in which he had confined himself. To be more exact, I consider Alford mistaken on the practical level, since Marcuse's article on Bahro did not offer an effective new strategy for implementing the true revolution. On the theoretical level, however, there is a logical way out of Marcuse's dilemma, and a very simple one at that. One need only demonstrate which elements can occur both before and after the revolution. Romanticism as revolutionary conservatism is one such element, since it is possible to say of Marcuse, as Martin Buber said of Gustave Landauer: "Ultimately what he has in mind is revolutionary conservatism: a revolutionary choice of the elements of the social being that are worth preserving and that are valid in a new construct."[33] Seen in this light, romanticism, far from being a paradox or a mark of resignation, is one among a number of factors of change. It must be understood that romanticism conforms to the revolutionary spirit and is not to be rejected where the interpretation of Marcuse is concerned.

Some writers have not understood this distinction. Eric Volant, in a thesis submitted to the University of Montreal, was a case in point.[34] After reminding his readers that "during debates at the Berlin Free University, Marcuse described himself as 'an incurable and sentimental romantic,' " he went on to say that Marcuse did not belong to the romantic tradition because his argument was based on the future.[35] Volant also attempted to contradict John Razer's analogy between Marcuse and the European romantic tradition, which appeared in "A Conversation with Herbert Marcuse" in *Psychology Today*.[36] Brigitte Croisier, when only a student in 1969, was aware of Marcuse's romanticism.[37] Yet commentators nevertheless persist in turning a blind eye to it. Michel de Certeau, commissioned by the *Encyclopaedia Universalis* to prepare an entry on Marcuse for *Universalia 1980*,[38] had reservations similar to those of Volant. While Marcuse's philosophy, said de Certeau, could be construed as "revolutionary romanticism," it probably originated in the Jewish tradition to which he belonged.[39] Marcuse had nevertheless denied this explicitly. In a conversation with Richard Kearney, he stated that the qualitative change he proposed was certainly aesthetic, but had nothing whatever to do with the messianic optimism of Judaism.[40]

What, then, is the meaning of the revolutionary romanticism to which Marcuse laid claim? Among the definitions of romanticism that come closest to the truth, stated H. Peyre in *Encyclopaedia Universalis*, "are those that emphasize its inherent spirit of revolt: not only the metaphysical revolt already evident in certain German writers and in Rousseau when he cried out against the suffocating limitations of the universe; but also social and political revolt."[41] The term romanticism in this context does not mean a particular literary genre, but a social and political vision of the world. The romantic figure is one who tries to change the world, said Hegel.[42] According to Jean-Michel Palmier, "Generally speaking, any action that violently contests the existing order in the name of ethical, aesthetic, or instinctual demands is an act of 'revolutionary romanticism.' "[43] Romanticism as a negation of established order is therefore to be found at the basis of all art. It is this thesis that Marcuse developed in *One-Dimensional Man*,[44] as Michel Haar noted.[45] But to what extent can art be revolutionary? Marcuse replied that it must transcend, without eliminating, all particular class content.[46] We are therefore dealing with two levels of consideration: the proletarian and the revolutionary. The question is, what are the respective preconditions of proletarian and revolutionary art from the Marxist standpoint?

In the eighth and final section of Marcuse's study on "Art and Revolution," Marcuse asked point blank if proletarian art were possible. What is "the meaning and the very possibility of a 'proletarian literature' (or working class literature)"?[47] Richard Kearney asked almost the same question in his interview,[48] and Marcuse replied in more or less the following terms. Let us presuppose the existence of a proletarian culture; one must also demonstrate that the proletariat as described by Marx himself does in fact exist, since today's working class is not always and everywhere interested in socialism. Even supposing that a proletarian socialism actually exists, it still must be shown that this can be the definite negation of capitalism. Marcuse clearly did not think so. Consequently, efforts to demonstrate that the working class would care about an authentic, radical, socialist art would only increase the already prevalent atmosphere of alienation.

Proletarian art is therefore impossible for several reasons, the first and foremost of which stems from the universal nature of art, as Marcuse explained in answer to another of Richard Kearney's questions.[49] Art can transcend any particular class interest without eliminating it. Art is always concerned with history—the history of *all classes*. It is this all-embracing quality that accounts for the objectivity and universality of art, which Marx described as the quality of "prehistory," and Hegel as the "continuity of substance"—the truth that links the modern novel with the medieval epic, the reality of human existence with its potentiality, and conflict with reconciliation, whether between man and man or man and nature. A work of art clearly has a particular class content in that it reflects a vision of a particular world, whether feudal, bourgeois, or proletarian. In terms of the human dream, however, it is transcendent. Genuine art does much more than mirror one class, and is not limited to the spontaneous expression of the frustrations or desires of a single group. The immediate sensuous impact of art, which popular culture does not always apprehend and which only the initiated can appreciate, presupposes the formal organization of experience on universal principles, and it is these principles alone that give a work any meaning that is not purely private. It is interesting to note that the most politically radical people often have apolitical tastes—yet further proof of the universality of art.

The notion of proletarian art is also doomed to failure, according to Marcuse, because it presupposes the obsolescence of earlier forms of art, classical as well as romantic. Unlike Herbert Read, he did not see classicism and romanticism as opposites. For Read, "There is a principle of life, of creation, of liberation, and that is the romantic spirit. There is a principle of order, of control and of repression, and that is the classical spirit."[50] Neither did Marcuse confuse classicism with capitalism.[51] He considered the disruptive characters of bourgeois literature, such as the prostitute, the great criminal, the rebel poet, the fool, and others, as representing a negative force confronting the Establishment.[52] Although this literature is not proletarian, it retains its revolutionary dimension, and this was what counted for Marcuse.

Present-day artistic realism, however, appears to have lost its revolutionary dimension. This is surely true of current protagonists, who often appear in the guise of beatnik, neurotic housewife, star, business tycoon, and the like. "They are no longer images of another way of life but rather freaks or types of the same life, serving as an affirmation rather than negation of the established order," wrote Marcuse.[53] In this respect the list is long: in the United States the songs of the black community have been swallowed up in white rock music; the indiscriminate use of scatological terms does more harm than good to sexual liberation; "living theater" or "anti-art," which has taken root in the spontaneous feelings of the oppressed proletariat, is doomed to failure, and so on *ad infinitum*.

Basically, Marcuse believed that proletarian art, if it exists, has lost its revolutionary potential because the majority of the working class has developed an antirevolutionary consciousness.[54] This being the case, can there still be a relationship between art and revolution?

Why should future revolutions be concerned with aesthetics if they wish to succeed? Marcuse considered it evident that the advanced industrial nations have long since reached the degree of productivity and wealth that Marx counted on as a base for building a socialist society. It therefore follows that quantitative growth in production no longer provides a sufficient goal, and that society as a whole must change qualitatively. Merely altering working conditions is not enough. "The qualitative change necessary to build a truly socialist society, something we haven't yet seen, depends on other values not so much economic (quantitative) as aesthetic (qualitative) in character."[55] In other words, it is not enough merely to satisfy needs; the needs themselves must be changed. This is how the new society can become a work of art.

But can one really consider art as an agent of revolution? Marcuse faced a genuine dilemma in this regard. Art is both affirmative and negative. Its essentially negative, critical nature is seen in the refusal of art to obey the rules of established reality in terms of language, order, conventions, and images. Art offers asylum to disreputable humanity, providing an alternative to the reality asserted by the Establishment. It can be used to denounce not only the affirmed reality, but those responsible for the affirmation. Paradoxically, however, art is also affirmative by nature. Literature, for example, is affirmative in that it gives pleasure to the reader—otherwise there would be no reader. The element of entertainment is part and parcel of even the most radical art. Like Bertolt Brecht, Marcuse made the point that even when describing the most brutal things in the world, one must still entertain.[56] Actually, a work of art can acquire an affirmative content through its social and political character, whereas it remains negative by virtue of its form (novel, play, or poem), which is forever demonstrating its removal from reality. Art always transforms reality. "No matter how realistic, naturalistic, it remains *the other* of reality and nature."[57]

If art can liberate us from the domination of reality—that is to say, if it can be revolutionary—then why did Marx not say so? The answer is simply this: Marx did not emphasize the role of art in the transition to a new society because he lived over a hundred years ago, and could not see for himself that it is indeed possible to resolve material problems through genuine socialist relations and institutions. He did not realize that a purely economic solution would not suffice, nor did he perceive that a twentieth-century revolution would require a different type of human being, striving for totally new personal and sexual relations, new morality, new sensitivity, and total reconstruction of the environment. All these values, in the name of which the revolution must be carried out, are in fact aesthetic values in the large sense used in *Eros and Civilization*, and in the tradition of Kant and Schiller. That is why art is an important factor in change.

It now becomes clear that the subtitle of Marcuse's last work, *Toward a Critique of Marxist Aesthetics*, was far from indicating a late and unexpected development of his thought—or resignation, as has been suggested. On the contrary, adhering to his own logic until the end, he continued his search for all possible means of revolution. He refused to countenance the form of Marxist orthodoxy that reduces all cultural phenomena to an ideological reflection of class interests, or that expects art to reflect the production relations of a given society and assumes that art and social classes are necessarily linked. Seen from the latter perspective, art and society are closely related; political and aesthetic values coincide so that only the highest social class is capable of true artistic expression, while the lowest can only produce decadent art. Artistic realism is the only form of art that mirrors society, according to this argument. Such a conception of art makes no allowance for variety of subject matter, personal feelings, or imagination, and equates individual consciousness to class consciousness. Marcuse, on the other hand, submitted the following thesis: "The radical qualities of art, that is to say, its indictment of the established reality and its invocation of the beautiful image (*schöner Schein*) of liberation are grounded precisely in the dimensions where art *transcends* its social determination and emancipates itself from the given universe of discourse and behavior while preserving its overwhelming presence."[58] He opposed cultural determinism and made out a case for autonomy in art, giving it a more important role and an enhanced political function. Instead of limiting himself to describing art in present-day society, he attempted to define its potential in the society of the future. For Marcuse, the world of art embodied "the promise of liberation."[59]

One may ask, however, whether Marcuse's critique is as relevant as he made it out to be, and whether it did not represent an outmoded school of thought. He himself admitted that he was dealing with a theory current between 1920 and 1935,[60] meaning the work of Walter Benjamin, Ernst Bloch, Bertolt Brecht, Georg Lukács, and several others. It was with Lukács that he differed especially, however. Unlike the latter, Marcuse argued that literature cannot realistically reflect objective social reality: "But precisely this requirement offends the very nature of art. The basic structure and dynamic of society can never find sensuous, aesthetic expression: they are, in Marxian theory, the essence behind the appearance, which can only be attained through scientific analysis, and formulated only in the terms of such an analysis."[61] Nevertheless, by taking up an antirealist position, Marcuse would seem to be abandoning the only perspective Marxism had to offer at the time. Gerald Graff remarked on this, pointing out that one cannot dismiss such American theorists as Edmund Wilson, Richard Chase, Irving Howe, Harold Rosenberg, Kenneth Burke, Philip Rahv, Alfred Kazin, Isaac Rosenfield, and Lionel Trilling.[62] Annette Rubinstein had much to say in the same vein, noting that Marcuse completely ignored current writing on Marxist aesthetics by Robert Weimann in the German Democratic Republic, Arnold Kettle in England, Zdanek Strbrny in Czechoslovakia, and others in such countries as Poland and Hungary.[63] In short, contrary to the thinking of early twentieth-century Marxist aestheticians, and without reference to those of the present day, Marcuse declared it an error to think that only proletarian literature can develop a revolutionary consciousness. The objectives and conditions of a revolution against monopolistic world capitalism cannot be expressed in terms of a proletarian revolution. "It is by means of the aesthetic imagination that one can transcend one's alienated world, in order to 'experiment' with and 'remember' alternative forms of life."[64] What, then, is the function of aesthetic philosophy?

Invited to chair a meeting of the American Philosophical Association,[65] Marcuse delivered a paper on Marx's eleventh thesis on Feuerbach: "Philosophers have only *interpreted* the world in various ways; the point is to *change* it." Marcuse contended: "This never meant that now it is no longer necessary to interpret the world—we can just go about changing it." What it really meant was, "The world must be interpreted again in order to be changed."[66] During an interview with Pierre Viansson-Ponte for the newspaper *Le Monde*, he commented on the eleventh thesis in slightly different terms: "It is the intellectual's job to promote radical education."[67] In other words, one has a moral duty to promote any theory that can be used for social subversion. Marcuse felt this duty to be all the more imperative because philosophical theory and all forms of critical thought are today facing a greater task than ever, since historical conditions tend to silence the spirit of criticism. Philosophy underlies the will to transform the world and make it free and rational, Marcuse pointed out. Its task cannot end until its goal is reached. Philosophy has not achieved its goal, however, since theory and practice do not yet coincide. Even though the philosopher may realize that unity of theory and practice is a purely utopian goal, he must never stop working for it until this end is attained.[68] Philosophers, said Marcuse, "should be worthy" of the compliment implied by Marx's statement that philosophy is "the head of the emancipation of man."[69] It should perhaps be noted that Marcuse conveniently omitted the rest of the quotation—"It's *heart* is the *proletariat*"[70]—thereby downplaying the role of the proletariat in realizing the goals of philosophy. Be that as it may, Marcuse's reexamination of Marxism didn't stop there. He looked at another well-known thesis, to which he gave a new direction. Marx stated, "It is not the consciousness of men that determines their being, but, on the contrary, their social being that determines their consciousness."[71] Elsewhere he expressed it as, "It is not consciousness that determines life, but life that determines consciousness."[72] In fact, wrote Marcuse, "With the possibility of the revolution being a 'qualitative leap' comes the appropriate dialectic for historical materialism—the idealistic core that was always there. The determination of consciousness through social assistance undergoes a change. Based on an economy aimed at eliminating poverty and exploitation, *it is the liberated consciousness that would determine the social being.*"[73]

Marcuse was therefore proposing a philosophy that was both materialistic and idealistic: "materialistic to the extent to which it preserves *in its concepts* the full concreteness, the dead and living matter of the social reality; . . . idealistic in as much as it analyzes this reality in the light of its 'idea,' that is, its real possibilities."[74] However, the element of 'idealism' present in historical dialectic assumed such dimensions that, when discussing the topic in *Reason and Revolution*, he concluded, "Theory will preserve the truth even if revolutionary practice deviates from its proper path. Practice follows the truth, not vice versa."[75]

Marcuse never abandoned "this faith in the primacy of correct theory," stated Martin Jay.[76] He was always concerned about preserving the primacy of reason, although he must surely have been aware of another famous Marxist thesis: "Not criticism but revolution is the driving force of history, also of religion, of philosophy and all other kinds of theory."[77] In an affluent society such as ours, however, revolution is impossible.[78] It is only possible when based on poverty. Therefore reason has only one function left, that of recalling both the poverty and the highest aspirations of the past, because "the authentic utopia is grounded in recollection."[79] Where are we to look for such aspirations? "In philosophy," said Marcuse, for this is where "traditional theory developed concepts oriented to the potentialities of man lying beyond his factual status."[80] One must be careful, however, not to exaggerate the importance of conceptual thought. Marcuse considered it useful only in that philosophy is the basis of liberation. Even though philosophy may develop into critical theory, "the abyss between rational and present reality cannot be bridged by conceptual thought."[81]

What philosophy did Marcuse use in his process of reinterpretation? In his presidential address to the American Philosophical Association, he provided a clear answer in the form of a four-point program.[82] He recommended that several areas of the history of philosophy be reinterpreted, beginning with Plato's demonstration of the best form of government, all too often subjected to ridicule. In addition, he asked philosophers to develop political linguistics, because language has become "an instrument of control and manipulation." He also suggested they investigate physiological and psychological epistemology through transcendental "rather than sociological analysis. Such analysis would differ from Kant" in that "forms of intuition" and "categories of understanding" would be treated as historical rather than pure. "These would be *a priori* because they would belong to the 'conditions of possible experience,' but they would be a *historical a priori* in the sense that their universality and necessity are defined (limited) by a specific, experienced historical universe." Marcuse also called for "the renewal of philosophical aesthetics." Note that he spoke of *philosophic aesthetics* and not *aesthetic philosophy*. Philosophy is limited to revealing the goals, values, and moral ideals that we should strive for, as ethics and religion have always done in the past. However, since all three disciplines are incapable of translating the said goals, values, and moral ideals into reality, this must be accomplished by other means. "Only art achieves it—in the medium of beauty."[83] Marcuse therefore gave aesthetics in general, and art in particular, a special status that philosophy does not possess, but which it has a duty to promote. Philosophy is concerned with the purposes and values governing human activity, or with what Marcuse understood by "the norms and aspirations which motivate the behavior of social groups in the process of satisfying their needs, material as well as cultural."[84] Through a process of politicization and a fresh analysis of human potential, philosophy can attempt to show how these eschatalogical aims can be transformed into real, aesthetic needs. As long as these aims and values do not become real needs, predicted Marcuse, the qualitative change between past and future society will not take place.[85] "By virtue of its historical position Marxian theory is in its very substance philosophy."[86] Marxian philosophy and aesthetics therefore share the common task of promoting the realization of beauty. "An animal," wrote Marx, "forms objects only in accordance with the standard and the need of the species to which it belongs, whilst man knows how to produce in accordance with the standard of every species, and knows how to apply everywhere the inherent standard to the object. Man therefore also forms objects in accordance with the laws of beauty."[87] Of what does this process of aestheticization consist? It must first be understood that Marcuse perceived and expressed modernity in terms of crisis.[88] Before discussing the social function of art and its ontological and historical position, I would therefore like to look at the problem of the "crisis of art."[89]

Philosophy is not yet obsolete, contended Marcuse. It has a task to perform: the promotion of aesthetics. The specific, basic aim of aesthetics is to subvert reality. How can art do this if it is constantly threatened by developing cultural conditions? In analyzing social reality, are we forced to consider "the end of art"? Can art possibly retain its independence? Jürgen Habermas asked Marcuse about this dilemma.[90] He pointed out that in "The Affirmative Character of Culture" written in 1937, Marcuse had asserted, "Beauty will find a new embodiment when it no longer is represented as real illusion but, instead, expresses reality and joy in reality. A foretaste of such potentialities can be had in experiencing the unassuming display of Greek statues or the music of Mozart or late Beethoven. Perhaps, however, beauty and its enjoyment will not even devolve upon art. Perhaps art as such will have no objects. For the common man it has been confined to museums for at least a century."[91] Now, said Habermas, Marcuse was defending another position, as in this statement from "Art and Revolution" in 1972: "The 'end of art' is conceivable only if men are no longer capable of distinguishing between true and false, good and evil, beautiful and ugly, present and future. This would be the state of perfect barbarism at the height of civilization—and such a state is indeed a historical possibility."[92] Habermas asked Marcuse what had led him to revise his initial theory. Marcuse replied that he still saw art as communication, but was now emphasizing its inherently critical nature for the very reason that this was its most threatened function. In fact, however, he approached the question from three different angles.

As Andrew Arato noted, Marcuse appeared to have changed his approach in response to a critique by Adorno.[93] In the 1937 essay on "The Affirmative Character of Culture," Marcuse followed the Marxist tradition, equating art too closely with ideology. In 1969, he interpreted the rebellion of the young intelligentsia as the dialectical cultural leap that makes art part of life.[94] With "Art and Revolution" in 1972, however, art was definitively geared to permanent aesthetic subversion: "The abolition of the aesthetic form, the notion that art could become a component of revolutionary (and prerevolutionary) *praxis*, until under fully developed socialism, it would be adequately translated into reality (or absorbed by 'science')—this notion is false and oppressive: it would mean the end of art."[95] Adorno's influence could not explain everything, however. There were more deep-seated reasons for Marcuse's change in outlook.

Where did Marcuse get his interest in art and aesthetics? In an interview with Bryan Magee he explained that he and the members of the Frankfurt School shared a critical perspective based on their justifiable and objective disillusionment with the progress of social change. Contrary to expectations, the incredible social wealth accumulated by the achievements of Western civilization in general, and capitalism in particular, have progressively hindered rather than helped the building of a more decent, humane society.[96] The language of art, however, provides a means of looking at reality from two vantage points. It stands outside established reality and the reality of everyday life; and it holds out the promise of a liberated world. The break with reality allows art to perform a critical function. It can be subversive as long as it maintains this break. If not, then we are facing the end of art. Even so, nothing can destroy the promise of happiness inherent in art. Marcuse recounted his personal reaction to these two dimensions of aesthetic experience in his lecture on "Art in the One-Dimensional Society."[97] The more he felt that traditional forms of artistic expression had lost their critical powers, the more despondent he became, foreseeing the end of art. Conversely, however, as more and more new forms of artistic expression appeared, he became increasingly hopeful. Then one day, while taking part in an anti-Vietnam demonstration where young people were singing the songs of Bob Dylan, he realized that this was the only revolutionary language left today.[98] If Marcuse learned anything from this experience, it was this: although one art form can overtake another that has lost its critical edge, the aesthetic form endures. A careful reading of various aesthetic analyses throughout Marcuse's career makes it clear how intertwined were the two strands of theory concerning the end and the autonomy of art. These analyses were constructed on a fairly basic system, and it is unnecessary to review them all in detail. I would, however, like to list their salient points.

Between 1934 and 1937, the Frankfurt School was interested in *mass culture*, as Martin Jay showed.[99] Marcuse's contribution was a condemnation of the "affirmative culture"[100] of contemporary Germany.[101] In 1958, he turned his attention to Soviet culture.[102] Between 1964 and 1967 he looked at the situation in the United States, his adopted country,[103] and in 1969 he evaluated the aesthetic/political aspect of the Paris student revolt of May 1968.[104] In 1972, he produced a critical study of the New Left and of his own aesthetics, making a clear distinction between "material culture" and "intellectual culture"[105] in order to analyze the "culture industry."[106] In 1977 he published the original German text of *The Aesthetic Dimension*, which appeared in English the following year. This was a final and highly critical review of Marxist aesthetics, as a preliminary to proposing a revised form—Marcusian aesthetics. At this juncture it is worth noting that the major French collection of his essays bears the title *Culture et société*, which expresses the underlying thrust of Marcuse's work better than the runaway bestsellers *Eros and Civilization*, *One-Dimensional Man*, or even *Repressive Tolerance*.

Let us look at one or two examples. Each time Marcuse considered the problem of art, culture, or aesthetics, he asked questions such as: What is their role under present historical conditions? Have they preserved their essential nature? Have they been assimilated by the socio-historic context? Upon careful consideration, it seems to me that these questions fall into three main categories: What is the socio-historical context with which we are dealing? Can art (or culture, or aesthetics) contest this socio-historical context, and if so, what is stopping it? Has art any real *chance* of contesting the socio-historical context?

In Germany, as Marcuse demonstrated in an article written in 1934,[107] Fascism had attempted to mobilize all levels of society in order to consolidate its political interests. He therefore spoke out against the decline of bourgeois culture in the face of National Socialism, asserting that "the greatest intellectual heritage of German history" must be preserved by being absorbed "in scientific social theory and the critique of political economy," although he felt that the prospect was "clouded with uncertainty."[108]

The Soviet Union was distinctive, as Marcuse pointed out in *Soviet Marxism*, in that the state controlled economic development, contrary to capitalist countries where the economy controlled the state.[109] By nationalizing socio-economic interests, the Soviet state stifled effective opposition, so that "the ideological sphere which is remotest from the reality (art, philosophy), precisely because of its remoteness, becomes the last refuge for the opposition to this order."[110] Nevertheless, art retains its transcendent, "critical cognitive function: to sustain the image of freedom against a denying reality."[111]

> On its deepest level, art is a protest against that which is. By that very token, art is a "political" matter. . . . But art as a political force is art only in so far as it preserves the images of liberation; in a society which is in its totality the negation of these images, art can preserve them only by *total refusal.*[112]

What real chance has art to hold its own in the Soviet context? The avowed aim of Soviet aesthetics is to reflect reality in the form of artistic images. "In other words," said Marcuse, "once the reality itself embodies the ideal, . . . art must necessarily reflect the reality."[113] Aesthetic realism is the only form of art permitted in the Soviet Union. Even though Marcuse felt that art should indeed try to reflect the ideal, he criticized Soviet aesthetics on three counts. In the first place, the reality does not yet embody the ideal "in its pure form."[114] Furthermore, "In its societal function, art shares the growing impotence of individual autonomy and cognition."[115] Finally, "The works of the great 'bourgeois' antirealists and 'formalists' are far deeper committed to the idea of freedom than is socialist and Soviet realism."[116]

In the United States Marcuse took a similar approach. In *One-Dimensional Man*, he contended that American capitalism has produced a closed society because the forces of opposition predating capitalism have been integrated. Assimilation is complete: the system "swallows up or repulses all alternatives;" negation and criticism are reduced to cohesion and affirmation.[117] "The world of facts is, so to speak, one-dimensional."[118] Marcuse continued to develop this idea, first put forward in 1936, including it in his course at the Ecole pratique des hautes études in 1958-59.[119] He worked on it again in articles published in 1961 and 1962, later to become passages in *One-Dimensional Man*, published in 1964.[120] Generally, his writing on one-dimensionality leads one to believe that his theory went from being a mere stalking horse to an all-pervading idea: the growth of rationality engenders a corresponding growth in irrationality. To combat the latter, however, Marcuse still posited the "total refusal" of 1958,[121] the aesthetic "Great Refusal."[122] Aesthetic values are the definite negation of dominant values, he asserted.[123] But the assimilative force of capitalist society is so great that even aesthetic imagination merges with reality.[124] This is "the end of art"—a theme taken from Hegel by all the exponents of critical theory.[125]

Hegel is the key to understanding "the end of art." He considered all theoretical and practical endeavour to be based on introspective thought. Liberated subjective consciousness thus adopts a stance opposed to socio-historical reality, creating a gap that art can no longer bridge, even by reconciling extremes. Marcuse, on the contrary, held that it was important to base oneself on an ethical/aesthetic ideal, an "illusory reality that neither philosophy nor religion can attain. Only art achieves it—in the medium of beauty."[126] He was therefore not prepared to accept the theory of "the end of art" as being the last word, and instead looked to the "autonomy of art." It was Habermas who touched on the real issue, however, when he asked whether Marcuse had generally revised his thinking on the "end of art" to the point of opting for the "autonomy of art." What distinguishes these two viewpoints is how each relates to revolution. When art is assimilated by the Establishment, it contributes to its own end. When, on the contrary, it recognizes its revolutionary potential and revives "the categorical imperative: 'things must change,' "[127] then art, by its very function, acquires and maintains autonomy. What, therefore, is the function of art in Marcuse's aesthetics?

Utopia and art have similar functions in Marcuse's critical theory. These can be examined in a number of ways. We can study Marcuse's ethical perspective for consistency of approach. We can look at the functions of critical theory, as resumed by Vincent Geoghegan in his 1981 work, *Reason and Eros, The Social Theory of Herbert Marcuse.*[128] We can also examine the functions of utopia, as outlined by Ernst Bloch, the utopian philosopher *par excellence*,[129] and by Paul Ricoeur, a much less enthusiastic commentator of concrete utopia.[130] In addition, there are the contemporary functions of Marxist utopia described by Pavel Kovaly,[131] and the function of art in Marcuse and Hegel, as given in George Friedman's recent work, *The Political Philosophy of the Frankfurt School.*[132]

The consistency of Marcuse's aesthetic perspective throughout his work has been the subject of comment more than once. François Chirpaz, for example, came to the following conclusion in 1969: "Marcuse's strong point is that he invites us to think in terms of a radical transformation of our society and culture; but he is nevertheless unable to provide the theoretical tools for planning and realizing such a transformation. In fact, *it is within the scope of aesthetic utopia* to expect such a transformation, considering the advances that have been made in automation, not to mention the emergence of new needs."[133] There is no doubt that Marcuse wanted to make use of an aesthetic utopia. Why then reproach him for having done so? Whatever else it may be, it is not inconsistent.

In a more recent study in 1977, Parviz Piran contended that Marcuse's approach differed from that of critical theory.[134] Piran claimed that the revolutionary change sought by Marcuse contradicted the change implied by his aesthetic perspective. Furthermore, on the basis of *One-Dimensional Man*, one might agree with Michel Haar's statement that, "If it is true that technology represents violence and repression, then it is utopian to base the advent of a world without violence and repression on technology."[135] But are these actually contradictions in Marcuse's theory, or real contradictions that Marcuse was trying to evaluate from a Marxist perspective?

For the sake of argument, let us use Roger Garaudy's definition of the Marxist perspective: The vantage point from which we can see all the avenues of Marx's thought is his awareness of man's basic situation in capitalist society. Marx enunciated the inherent contradiction of this situation, which is that the birth and growth of capitalism have created conditions for both the unlimited development and oppression of all men.[136]

If, therefore, the Marxist perspective consists in demonstrating society's contradictions, and if this is what Marcuse did on the aesthetic level, then one cannot argue that his thought is confined to the contradictions of the capitalist world. For example, although Marcuse advocated a radical aesthetic education, he considered it obvious that the present concept of education, designed to promote a better future society, is a *contradiction*. However, it is a contradiction that must be resolved if progress is to be made.[137] This last assertion was not an admission of weakness on his part, but rather the expression of a desire to benefit humanity. Marcuse tended to express society's contradictions in pairs, juxtaposing them to a third, utopian element of his argument, located outside of present time and space so as to avoid setting arbitrary limits to the historical process.

The consistency of Marcuse's thought was evident, for example, in the following pairs of opposites: total refusal versus one-dimensionality; the autonomy of art versus the possibility of the end of art; and non-repressive sublimation versus repressive desublimation. Critical theory was the only intellectual bridge he offered to span the gap between one historical moment and another. What, then, are the functions of critical theory?

Vincent Geoghegan considered the functions of critical theory to be threefold: it *sets forth* the present historical situation; it *reveals* the inherent possibilities of this situation; and it *anticipates* the future by emphasizing the role of imagination. These functions are, in fact, surprisingly like those of utopia itself.[138]

Ernst Bloch also summarized the functions of utopia according to three principals, as listed by Pierre Furter and Laënnac Hurbon. Utopia is the *protest* against the status quo; the *anticipation* of the possibilities of radical change; and the *insistence on realizing everything* immediately, which constitutes a refusal of defeatism.[139]

Ernst Bloch was not the only utopian philosopher to outline these functions, however. Paul Ricoeur, although not a particular supporter of utopia, proposed using it as a means of *refuting* the threat of meaningless existence.[140] "The basic function of utopia is to *maintain a project* for humanity in the face of meaninglessness," he wrote.[141] In another article, he enlarged upon this idea: "I believe . . . there is an historic function of utopia in the social order. Only utopia can give to economic, social and political action a human intention and, in my sense, a double intention: on the one hand the will of humanity as a totality; on the other hand, the will of the person as a singularity."[142]

In general, Ricoeur considered it the task of the educator to be utopian.[143] On the strictly political level, he explained, the intellectual is responsible for offering a social project geared to both general and individual human needs, and capable of maintaining a healthy balance between the ethics of conscience and the ethics of responsibility.[144]

How does this view of utopian functions compare with the Marxist approach? Let us look at Paul Kovaly's critique of the contemporary functions of Marxist utopia.[145] He based it on a statement by Adam Schaff, head of the Institute of Philosophy and Sociology at the University of Warsaw, and one of the most influential Polish socialist writers. Schaff said, "Reading the classic Marxist texts on man under communism one sometimes gets the feeling that they are utopian. No doubt they contain a residue of utopia."[146] Kovaly felt that it was not enough, however, simply to admit that Marxism contained utopian elements. One must also understand how utopia functions in social and political life, and ask whether it affects society as a whole.

The ultimate goal assigned by Marx and Engels to future society may be grand, noble, and just. However, this ideal goal has become the unique criterion by which Marxists judge and evaluate both individual actions and social movements. All means and methods are considered as serving this goal. At this juncture, utopia becomes dystopia. "I think that Marxism can be a very good tool of analysis—but a dangerous tool when it is taken as a theory of totality," stated Ricoeur.[147] The social phenomenon, whether viewed as civilization or culture, is better understood if a distinction is made among levels of reality, instead of systematizing every aspect of existence. It is not as though we had no format for discussing historical totality. On the contrary, our historical experience seems to affect everything in our lives. But every imaginable totality is always premature or else merely a limitation of the historical process.

The Marxist utopia may suffer from a monolithic structure that makes it difficult to develop in more than one direction, but this does not lessen the importance of its utopian function. In a passage on the constituent function of utopia, Ricoeur explained that, in social theory, the fiction of another society allows us to distance ourselves from reality and discover how strange it seems from another perspective. Through utopia, he said, man distances himself from his symbolical system, thereby putting all his institutions into question; in other words, he rethinks his status as a political animal.[148]

Unlike Ricoeur, Marcuse saw aesthetic utopia as playing a far more important role. The functions of critical theory and art are similar, he maintained. In fact, he used this premise to define a work of art in the last section of *One-Dimensional Man*:

> Like technology, art creates another universe of thought and practice against and within the existing one. But in contrast to the technical universe, the artistic universe is one of illusion, semblance, *Schein*. However, this semblance is resemblance to a reality which exists as the threat and promise of the established one. In various forms of mask and silence, the artistic universe is organized by the images of a life without fear . . . . The more blatantly irrational the society becomes, the greater the rationality of the artistic universe.[149]

As George Friedman so aptly expressed it, Marcuse reworked the Hegelian notion of the status and function of art.[150] The work of art maintains a critical relation with the actual world in order to create a reasonable desire for the beautiful, which could destroy the ugliness of the real world through practical politics.

When the work of art can no longer preserve its critical stance and offer a viable alternative to the irrationality of the world, it is assimilated; it becomes an affirmation instead of a negation of the existing world. This is virtually the end of art. It cannot regain its autonomy, according to Marcuse, unless it becomes politically involved. The difficulty here is that the aestheticization of politics may conceal the pitfall of Plato's radical aestheticism.

The members of the Frankfurt School were united in their belief that art and life are intimately linked.[151] Their goals differed widely, however. Horkheimer was interested in religion, but Benjamin, Adorno, and Marcuse continued to explore art, although from different angles.

Art and politics can be related to one another in many ways. The philosophical question of their relations is nothing new. Nevertheless, present historical conditions have forced us to put the question in special terms, according to Benjamin.[152] Briefly, there seem to be two possible relations: either politics determines art, as in Communism; or art determines politics, as in Fascism. In other words, either art is subordinated to politics as in Communist societies, so that the work of art loses its unique character and is watered down into art for the masses; or else an attempt is made to aestheticize politics, as in Fascist societies, and to force an aesthetic ideal on the masses. For Benjamin, the alternatives appeared so repugnant that he preferred a melancholy retreat into metaphysics.[153] Adorno, on the other hand, took the Fascist threat seriously, but was unable to resign himself as Benjamin had, and consequently sought to preserve the work of art's capacity for negation.[154] Marcuse, however, took Adorno's position to its logical conclusion. By recognizing the cognitive function of imagination, he restored a "repressed harmony."[155] Through harmony, as preserved in the work of art, he wanted to organize social reality to the point where society itself became a work of art.

Here I would like to digress briefly and ask, as did Friedman, why Benjamin occasionally flirted with socialist realism. Moreover, why did Marcuse take up positions that, by implication, admitted the possibility of dictatorship? Perhaps there is no answer to such questions, but Friedman raised an interesting hypothesis, all the same. He felt that each seemed to have rejected what he understood best—Benjamin, Fascism, and Marcuse, Soviet Communism. Each accepted the unacceptable because the alternative seemed the greater evil.[156]

Let us return now to the idea of society as a work of art, an idea that goes back to Plato, and one that Marcuse held dear. Both shared a radical aestheticism that deserved the criticism leveled at it by Karl Popper. For Marcuse, the construction of the ideal society was based on a new science, a "science of the Imagination,"[157] a science that must be the principal guide to social and political action,[158] a "science of the beautiful" and "of redemption and fulfillment"[159] that, taken to its limits, would become art.[160] Plato said that "a king's government is a *science*" and "an *art*,"[161] Popper noted. Indeed, Plato was of the view that politicians, like artists, should work on a clean canvas.

> No State can be happy which is not designed by artists who imitate the heavenly pattern . . . . They will begin by taking the State and the manners of men, from which, as from a tablet, they will rub out the picture, *and leave a clean surface*. This is no easy task. But whether easy or not, herein will lie the difference between them and every other legislator,—they will have nothing to do either with individual or State, and will inscribe no laws, until they have either received from others, or themselves made, a clean surface.[162]

How are we to interpret this idea of making "a clean surface"? Popper's answer followed the principles laid down by Plato.[163] The "authorities" must, "by the application of *science* and *justice*" create the best possible state, even if they have to use "executions or sentences of banishment" to do so.[164] This seems oddly reminiscent of the prison to be demolished before building the house,[165] and the justifications of revolutionary violence advocated by Marcuse.

The extreme positions adopted by Plato and Marcuse cannot withstand Popper's two arguments, which may be summed up as follows. To begin with, when Plato called for a clean surface and Marcuse advocated demolishing the prison before building the house, they meant that the existing social system must be destroyed. The trouble with this is that both painter and architect belong to the system, and will therefore destroy themselves and their utopian plans as well. They would need an Archimedes' fulcrum outside of society to obtain the required leverage—something that only exists in imagination. Secondly, romantic aestheticism leads to the sacrifice of reason in exchange for a desperate faith in political miracles.[166] It should be noted here that both philosophic and literary romanticism go back as far as Plato, who clearly influenced Rousseau. Kant recognized in Rousseau a romantic obscurantism, despite his admiration for the *Social Contract*.

No discussion of Platonic and Marcusian radical aesthetics would be complete without an explanation of why it is particularly appropriate that Popper's arguments be used to refute them. The Marcuse-Popper debate was one of the many controversies that have enlivened German sociology over the years. First there was the controversy led by Max Weber on the axiological neutrality of the social sciences. Next came the positivist controversy between Adorno and Popper, later the debate between Hans Albert and Jürgen Habermas, and finally that between the latter and Arnold Gehlen regarding values in the social sciences.[167]

The one point I should like to make is that I agree with Popper in favoring clear, written commentary over Marcuse's voluntary confessions or avowals. To illustrate, let us compare the respective statements of Popper and Marcuse on Adorno. Popper criticized Adorno's writing style because it was confusing. When Adorno wrote (in German), "Totality has no existence outside of that to which it gives cohesion, and in which its components are to be found," he could have simply said that society consists of social relations.[168] In contrast, Marcuse remarked of Adorno (also in German), "His language is excessive because of the fear of succumbing to reification, . . . the fear of being too easily understood and becoming familiar and therefore misunderstood. I must admit that Adorno's sentences have often enraged me, . . . but I think that is what they're supposed to do. And I don't think I need be ashamed of it."[169]

In an interview with Marcuse, Bryan Magee spoke of the difficulty of reading work by the Frankfurt School in general. At times Magee found them unintelligible—particularly Adorno. He therefore asked Marcuse's opinion, knowing that Marcuse considered Adorno a true genius. Marcuse replied that he agreed with Magee to a point, admitting that there were several passages in Adorno that he did not understand. He excused Adorno, however, on the grounds that there was a possible danger in prematurely popularizing the terrible and complex problems of today.[170]

I must admit that I share Marcuse's reservations in this respect. Language can distance us from the real world. It can isolate us from the world of things unless we are seeking to make contact through philosophy. If I choose Popper and reform rather than Marcuse and revolution, it is not to exclude Marcuse, but in fact to include him. In the final decades of the twentieth century, I think nothing is more important than being able to understand Marcuse's discussion of the "end." Can theory ever be the same after Auschwitz? And does not the real possibility of humanity's nuclear destruction force us to find new means of expression? The answer is yes, and this is what Marcuse understood in his way. It is important now and for the foreseeable future to comprehend Marcuse's apocalyptic message, his cry of despair. He pushed his theory to the limit, to the point where it became an urgent warning. And if we follow the reasonable course of maximal reform instead of universal revolution (which Marcuse admitted was impossible), we do not thereby deny the importance of dialectical imagination, aesthetic or otherwise. The Popper-Marcuse controversy must not make us forget the true debate of the twentieth century. This is the inspiration we should derive from Popper, who said, "I assuredly do not think that the debate about social reform must be confined to those who begin by demanding that they be recognized as practical revolutionaries, and who consider the only function of the revolutionary intellectual to be the deliberate flaunting of all that is most repugnant in our social life (outside their strictly sociological context)."[171]

It is my contention that reality is complex and that language, as part of reality, is equally complex. It must remain that way, to the extent that it reflects the intricacies of reality while attempting to enlighten it through knowledge. The existence of such knowledge is beyond question, because without it we would be in total darkness. It is for each one of us to enlighten reality as best we may, for the flicker of shadows on the wall of the cave is perhaps all we shall ever know.

IV

Marcuse's Ideological Politics

Inevitably, when we think of Marcuse the phrase "political liberation" comes to mind. Yet there seems to be widespread confusion as to what this phrase means, and more particularly, what Marcuse meant by it.

Martin Jay, in his article on Marcuse and "The Metapolitics of Utopianism," ended with the following words: "The political imperative that follows from all of this is the cul-de-sac of apocalyptic metapolitics, which is really no politics at all."[1] Jay's conclusion was correct, in my view. He had reached it after showing that the principal form of political action advocated by Marcuse was the Great Refusal. This involved the aestheticization of politics, which amounted to a complete rejection of the mechanisms of political change in the existing system. Rejection of present political mechanisms is easy to justify, since they all too often fail to live up to their promises. But a total and final refusal, without appeal, is in fact a rejection of politics itself. I cannot believe that politics is destined to disappear from our lives at some future period. Political activity is a basic, specific activity, which works toward a clearly determined goal and has its own dynamic. It is from this standpoint that I want to examine what Marcuse meant by political liberation, as well as discuss his political economy and evaluate his ideological politics.

Marcuse believed that everything today is political. The ultimate goal to which he dedicated himself was total emancipation of the human race and of the individual. Total emancipation therefore meant complete freedom from politics. "Political freedom would mean liberation of the individuals *from* politics over which they have no effective control," he asserted.[2] What we have to ask ourselves, however, is whether such a position implies a false conception of freedom, and whether it confuses *liberty* with *liberties*.

I feel it is important to be aware of the fundamental distinction between *liberty* and *liberties*. Raymond Aron, in his *Essai sur les libertés*, has reminded us of this distinction in his commentary on passages from Alexis de Toqueville.[3] The use of the notion of liberty in the singular has grown with the development of individualism in contemporary Western civilization. The problem was masterfully dealt with by C. B. Macpherson in *The Political Theory of Possessive Individualism* and *The Life and Times of Liberal Democracy*.[4] Let us consider, at this juncture, the distinction between the libertarian spirit, which seeks *liberty*, and the liberal spirit, which sees things in terms of *liberties*.

It is characteristic of the libertarian spirit to speak of liberty in the singular, a tendency that apparently goes back to the eighteenth century, when ideologies began to assume greater importance. Previous to this, people spoke of liberties in the plural, in the sense of freedoms or privileges. These two notions of liberty conceal an underlying opposition between the "libertarian spirit" and the "liberal spirit." Marcuse subscribed to a libertarian humanism, recognizing that "freedom is liberation."[5] But the desire for total liberation may carry with it the danger of freedom from liberty itself. What, therefore, is the most acceptible concept of liberty: liberty as liberation, liberties in the sense of specific feedoms, or liberty as an abstract, ideal concept?

Let us first consider *liberty as liberation*. Basically, this means total liberty, which presupposes the elimination of all religious, economic, and political alienation in the Marxist sense. There is a valid aspect to this concept of liberty. In my view, Marx was right to condemn the conditions of freedom created by the modern state and to denounce the mechanisms that enslave us to a brutally indifferent society. It is true to say that if liberty is not formally enshrined it will never contribute to human liberation. However, even though the criticism implied by the Marxist conception of liberty is accurate, it does not necessarily mean that we must uphold the dream of total liberation. By criticizing liberty as an abstract concept that can never be realized, and favoring liberation as a historical process to be implemented by a "transcendental project," Marcuse was elevating the very thing that Marx made a point of bringing down to earth, at least partially. Marcuse deliberately put liberty-as-liberation back on an eschatalogical plane, that is to say, he related it to a future or final goal. It was from the eschatological standpoint that he was interested in Marx's thought.[6]

The concept of *liberty in the plural*, on the other hand, seems to me to describe reasonably well the liberal spirit that sees a form of liberty for each human activity. These various forms of liberty compete with one another. Political freedom may curtail economic freedom. For the liberal spirit, the freedoms that matter are those which, although described as formal, have a concrete existence, such as freedom of speech, freedom of conscience, the right to free assembly, and so on. These concrete liberties can guarantee us a minimum of freedom, even if they cannot always provide the maximum. In politics, it is a mistake always to desire the ideal maximum and disdain the concretely possible.

Liberty in the singular, or in the abstract, is an ultimate goal. As such, its role is to orient human activity as a whole. Human activity can be inspired by *liberty* as a norm or model, but that is all. On this plane it will always be a project. What is involved is the final or eschatological goal which is the common denominator of all human activity. This, according to Julien Freund, can be clearly distinguished from other planes of finality: the teleological, which makes it possible to determine the specific goal of a given activity, and the technological, which is the level where concrete and limited objectives can be realized.[7] These distinctions, although formal in one sense, are nevertheless very useful in helping us understand reality—reality being always rather indistinctly perceived.

The same is true of the three-way distinction among liberty-as-liberation, liberties, and liberty in the singular. For one thing, it enables us to keep a clear mental picture of the difference between the elusive vision of total emancipation and the minimum of liberty to be gained through political activity. For the liberal spirit, what matters is that man should achieve the greatest possible liberty, despite the inevitable and inherent constraints of social life. This spirit deems that liberty is today part of the human condition. By contrast, the libertarian spirit, to which Marcuse subscribed, upholds the opposite view. It sees contemporary civilization as controlling all free activities such as economics, politics, ethics, and philosophy, and therefore blocking the genuine liberation made possible by technological progress through increased leisure. If man were not repressed, that is to say, obliged to conform to the system, he could exercise his creativity in any field he chose to. Man thinks he is economically free today because he can choose among a variety of products; but in the libertarian view this is not freedom. Politically there is no genuine freedom either, because government and opposition alike support the status quo. On the level of ethics, society is only superficially permissive; instincts are not really liberated, since sexuality, for example, has been integrated into the consumer society. As for intellectual activity, it has lost its critical powers to such an extent that only utopia can fill the vacuum. Real philosophy, that is, philosophy that has kept its liberating function, cannot escape the domination of facts except by becoming critical theory that paves the way for liberation, even though the forces of liberation may not exist in our time. Accordingly, Marcuse's critical theory was part and parcel of those theories of emancipation that ask man to hope for liberation in order to bring it about, thereby contributing to his future freedom. In other words, man is asked to wait for others in the future to take on the cause of his liberty . According to Marcuse, man can, in the present, actively choose to believe that maximum liberty is historically attainable in the here and now, despite the fact that the opposition portrays such liberty as utopian: "*The idea of a different form of Reason and Freedom, envisioned by dialectical idealism as well as materialism, appears again as Utopia. But the triumph of regressive and retarding forces does not vitiate the truth of this Utopia.* The total mobilization of society against the ultimate liberation of the individual, which constitutes the historical content of the present period, indicates how real is the possibility of this liberation."[8] But what chance of success does the historical process of liberation actually have, given—as Marcuse admitted—that "it has its right and wrong, its truth and falsehood"?[9]

This liberating process necessarily involves economics. But pure economics did not interest Marcuse. It was only Marxist political economics that attracted him. The focus of his attraction can be described in terms formulated by Roger Garaudy: "The central point, from which we get a panoramic view of all the avenues of Marxist thought, is our awareness of man's basic situation within capitalist society. Marx revealed the basic contradiction inherent in this situation: the birth and growth of capitalism have created both the conditions for unlimited expansion for all men, and the conditions of man's enslavement."[10]

How can the historical process overcome this contradiction? Institutions alone cannot achieve it. The men and women whose fate is affected by the process must be involved. Marx's materialist dialectic and his humanism unite in asserting that human growth and fulfilment can only come about through the realization of a historical possibility, outside of any metaphysical considerations. But how, we may ask, can political economics as such resolve the contradiction that has arisen "between the possibilities of unlimited human development and the *de facto* enslavement of the majority of human beings"?[11] Roger Garaudy's answer was as follows: "In speaking of man's relationship to nature, Marx, in his critique of political economics, evoked the hopes and failures of the Industrial Revolution implemented by capitalism, which created real possibilities while preventing their realization."[12] In theory, Marcuse turned his attention to this same contradiction. However, what Marx applied to industrial society, Marcuse reinterpreted for the new historical conditions produced by the technological development of what he termed "advanced industrial society." In *One-Dimensional Man*, for example, he explained this underlying contradiction of our civilization by showing how current technology is capable of creating conditions that would assure a peaceful existence, while this same technology is firmly entrenched in a status quo that conditions humans to continue the battle for survival and therefore to oppose any social alternative.[13] The idea that the productive forces which develop within the capitalist system destroy the potential for liberation was not new, since it was in line with traditional Marxism. As André Gorz pointed out, it was "one of Herbert Marcuse's central theses."[14] But Marcuse differed from orthodox Marxist tradition, not as to the existence of such a contradiction, but on how to overcome it. According to the orthodox view, the system must be fought from within. For Marcuse, however, the system could only be overcome from outside—from the utopian base of a non-repressive civilization made possible by scientific and technical development. "The End of Utopia" made it even more explicit. He began by admitting that "the notion of the end of utopia implies the necessity of at least discussing a new definition of socialism. The discussion would be based on the question of whether decisive elements of the Marxian concept of socialism do not belong to a new obsolete stage in the development of the forces of production."[15] He then added: "All the material and intellectual forces which could be put to work for the realization of a free society are at hand. That they are not used for that purpose is to be attributed to the total mobilization of existing society against its own potential for liberation."[16] Consequently, there was a difference between the old socialism of Marx and the new socialism of Marcuse. For Marx, the transition to a classless society was to be carried out through an intermediary stage, essentially the dictatorship of the proletariat. As a socialist, Marcuse considered utopia immediately realizable, explaining that "the unrealistic sound of these propositions is indicative, not of their utopian character, but of the strength of the forces which prevent their realization."[17]

Despite these divergences, Marcusian economics nevertheless belonged to the Marxist type. And like the latter, his economics assumed a sociological dimension that extended to the place and significance of economics in society as a whole. Before reviewing Marcusian economics, however, it would be helpful to take a brief look at Marcuse's perspective of society as a whole. This has been definitively outlined by George Kateb in his article "The Political Thought of Herbert Marcuse."[18] He reduced Marcuse's thinking to five theses:

> 1) advanced industrial society, or the affluent society, in the West, with the United States farthest along, is preponderantly evil, both for the harm it does and the good it prevents, internally and externally;
> 2) on balance, and internally, the Soviet Union is worse in actuality, better in potentiality, but with no guarantee that it will in fact become better;
> 3) the evil of each system is not correctable peacefully, by those in control or by their likely heirs;
> 4) in the abstract, revolution *may* therefore be justifiable;
> 5) we *may* be witnessing the emergence of certain forces that could perhaps bring about qualitative, genuinely revolutionary changes in the West, while developments in the Soviet bloc are, if anything, more problematic.

To round out this picture, I would like to add a further thesis. The "totalitarian" revolution,[19] which "may take all but a century,"[20] is at this moment impossible,[21] even if the utopia of a non-repressive civilization is realizable.[22]

The fact that Marcuse has a Marxist perspective meant that his economics involved seeking out basic economic contradictions that would "explode" society. As Marcuse said, "The revolutionary process always begins with and in economic crisis."[23] We can summarize his economic theories, as John Fry did,[24] in the following manner. The economy of advanced industrial society, and more especially of North American capitalist society, is prosperous and stable.[25] Externally, this stability is due to "a defense-based economy,"[26] a "war economy,"[27] or "the Western defense economy."[28] Internally, stability is assured by the ability to eliminate cyclical crises,[29] and to deal peacefully with class conflict by producing an ever-larger amount of commodities.[30] In such an economy, production is continually increasing because it can rely on accelerated technological development.[31] Distribution of goods is carried to the point of waste, profitable for some, detrimental to others.[32] The economic expansion of advanced industrial society is guaranteed, because it is able to contain the explosive situation caused by the gap between itself and the Third World.[33] It is all the more successful because the Third World is the only genuinely revolutionary force directed against it.[34] This force should serve as an example to the New Left,[35] even though, all things considered, it does not pose a serious threat.[36]

In Marcuse's view, these major contradictions ought to explode the system from within because, as he pointed out, "The notion that the liberating historical forces develop *within* the established society is a cornerstone of Marxian theory."[37] But this synthesis was far from proving that the system was likely to explode. On the contrary, it demonstrated its stability.

Why did Marcuse emphasize the stability of the North American economic system rather than show us the real weaknesses that could bring about its destruction? After all, this was one of the essential aims of his proposed revolution. In other words, why did he state that "the chain of exploitation must break at its strongest link"?[38] The answer is that Marcusian critical theory, although Marxist in type, differed widely from Marxist critical theory. The latter analyzed our alienation, while Marcuse described the "closing" of our political and intellectual universe. The philosophy of alienation, by revealing the workers' predicament, incites them to reject the conditions that cause it. But a philosophy of containment, which shows how contented workers are with their lot, cannot reveal the negative aspects of the system from within. This is why, wrote Marcuse, "qualitative change appears possible only as a change from *without*."[39] The many and obvious internal contradictions of the system are disappearing. Marxist theory taught us that poverty increased as wealth accumulated, whereas Marcuse pointed out that today the working class enjoys the advantages of progress through ever-increasing consumption. Marxist theory was based on class conflict, whereas Marcuse held that today classes are becoming so uniform that "the Marxian 'proletariat' is a mythological concept."[40] Consequently, only one contradiction remains, and it can only be seen by stepping outside the objectives of the present economic system. This contradiction involves the omnipresence of repression on one hand, and the real possibility of liberating ourselves on the other. Marcuse's economic theory cannot, therefore, offer us a collective, historical, and transcendent project.[41]

As a solution, Marcuse's non-competitive economy has numerous snares for the unwary, even though Marcuse held that it would be historically possible during the transition from a period of scarcity to a period of affluence. The fact is, we have been laboring under a misapprehension as to the nature of violence. For almost two centuries it was thought that violence was linked to an economic regime of scarcity, and inversely that the onset of a regime of affluence would provide a remedy. Not only Marx, but Frédéric Bastiat, Saint-Simon, and Auguste Comte believed it.[42] Our present experience, however, shows that they were mistaken. The great sociologists of the early twentieth-century, such as Emile Durkheim, Vilfredo Pareto, and Max Weber, forced us to recognize that violence in an affluent society, far from decreasing, finds new causes for erupting. However, we cannot therefore conclude that a period of affluence automatically produces greater violence. This would imply an intellectual confusion between economics and politics, since the satisfaction of needs is an economic consideration, whereas the containment of violence is political.

To expect politics to solve all economic problems would amount to politicism. But a politician's job is to supervise social organization so that human beings can live together for their maximum, mutual benefit, thereby permitting the greatest possible growth and fulfilment of each individual and group in all human activities—science, art, law, and so on.

If we reject politicism, then by implication we also reject ideologism, for another way of expressing the idea that "everything is politics" is to say that "everything is ideology." And yet it was all right for Marcuse to speak of ideology in the singular, as did Adorno, whom he quotes: "Nothing remains of ideology but the recognition of that which is—model [*sic*] of a behavior which submits to the overwhelming power of the established state of affairs."[43] To avoid the pitfalls of ideologism, however, we can make a point of speaking of ideologies in the plural, as recommended by Olivier Reboul at the beginning of *Langage et ideologie*: "When studying ideology, we ought only to use this term in the plural, and take care not to evaluate any particular one as though it were the only ideology."[44] It is interesting to note that we talk of Marcuse's ideological politics and not his ideology. Usage has confirmed this distinction between adjective and noun. As Reboul put it: "No one says, 'This is my ideology.' Some left wing parties do talk of their 'ideological battles,' it is true, but this is because the adjective has a less deprecatory connotation than the noun. It is as if the word 'ideology' referred not only to what is ideological, but to what is exclusively ideological."[45]

In order to avoid purely polemical considerations, I have not discussed Marcuse's ideology in the following pages. Instead, I have dealt with his ideological politics using Reboul's working definition, which combines those of Julien Freund and Jean Baechler.[46] To put it another way, I have consciously refused to use ideology as a purely negative term, because it has the positive function of enabling people to engage in discussion without violence. It is this positive aspect of ideology that Reboul propounded in his article *La Violence et l'idéologie*, which appeared two years before his book.[47] What, therefore, are the principal characteristics of Marcuse's ideological politics? And what reservations have we?

As William Leiss, John David Ober, and Erica Sherover have clearly expressed it, "The essential element of Marcuse's teaching is that knowledge is partisan."[48] It is a good thing for politics to be partisan in the sense that we are invited to take sides, *choice* being the first and foremost consideration. But what are the choices? We of course know, as Marcuse rightly said, that no society in history has been able to offer its members the full range of possibilities open to humankind. Ideally, the widest possible choice is offered. But in fact this is not what happens. Choices are limited. Some people try to make choices other than those offered by a given society in the here and now, appearing as partisans of the spirit of revolution. There is nothing intrinsically wrong with this. All shades of opinion have a right to be expressed, and all parties a right to be represented. We subscribe to the premise that pluralism offers the greatest number of choices. The range of choice, however, depends on one important condition: whether or not members of a given society can make contact with people from outside that society—with foreigners, in other words. For centuries, European civilization fulfilled this condition, because its basic drive since the Renaissance was to explore the universe. The Europe of our day, by contrast, seems to be faced with a kind of closed-door mentality in the sense that it has apparently reached the limit of its exploratory thrust. The result is a turning inward, or decadence.[49] No further outside contribution can revolutionize society. It is no longer sufficient to describe how some traveler fresh from foreign parts has brought a new model to stimulate a change in outlook. This is what Sir Thomas More did through the accounts of that inveterate gossip, Raphael Hythlodaeus (or Raphael Nonsenso, as Paul Turner rendered it in his Penguin Classics translation). Classic literary utopia has given way to a transcendent project, an indeterminate utopia which tells us to demolish our prison in order to build a house in its place, before we have the detailed blueprints for its construction.[50] We must first bring about the revolution, in other words, and put off until later the search for new ways to organize society. Marcuse was thus taking refuge in revolutionarism, or the belief in action for its own sake, the cult of action pure and simple. But instead of merely inviting us to take sides as any healthy politics would, even if it were a question of siding against the establishment, Marcuse retreated to ideological politics—politics that takes sides because, in addition to being partisan, it is also partial. The epigraphs chosen by Marcuse for the opening pages of *Philosophie et Révolution* testify eloquently to this. He uses two quotations from Feuerbach. The first states that in order to inaugurate a new era, humanity must make a clean break with the past: it must adopt the position that all that has gone before is, in principle, worthless; consequently it must occasionally throw out the baby with the bathwater; it must be unjust, partial.[51] The other is the thesis that practice will resolve those doubts which theory has been unable to solve.[52]

Marcuse's ideological politics were based on a future stand, this being one of the distinctive marks of revolutionary and/or utopian romanticism, as Michael Loewy has shown.[53] This form of politics sees history as progress, and tries to make us forget that politics should envisage the worst eventualities in order to avoid them. It attempts to convince us either that tomorrow's humanity will possess greater qualities, or else that today's humanity has lost all the great qualities it once had. While we can quite legitimately predict that our living conditions are continually improving in the light of technological development, it is far less legitimate to reduce our ancestors to mediocrities.

Politics are not only partisan, however. They have a polarizing effect, as Marcuse's short work, *Repressive Tolerance*, demonstrated. There is no room for intermediate views: everything is black or white. One claims to understand the theory or practice of everybody, even if nobody actually thinks or practices in a given way. One sees oneself, as Marcuse did, in various forms of expression, such as a slogan:

> I would like to take as a motto of my talk one of the inscriptions on the walls of the Sorbonne in Paris, which seems to mark the very essence of what is going on today. The inscription said, "Soyons réalistes, demandons l'impossible." Let us be realistic, let us ask for the impossible.

a popular song:

> I saw and participated in their demonstrations against the war in Vietnam, when I heard them singing the songs of Bob Dylan, I somehow felt, and it is very hard to define, that *this is really the only revolutionary language left today*.[55]

a movement:

> *Ideological differences* and divisons become utterly irrelevant and ridiculous when such a mass base has yet to be created.[56]

a distinctive aphorism:

> The classical alternative "socialism or barbarism" is more urgent today than ever before.[57]

or in relation to two mutually exclusive poles: for example, nationalism and revolution in the Weimar Republic,[58] to which Marcuse continually related himself.

In this way Marcuse believed he could escape what he referred to as the most vicious of today's ideologies, that which ridicules projections of a free society because it views such a society as speculative and utopian.[59]

The pressure on ideologies to justify their position is somewhat superfluous, considering that they are based on unshakable conviction and supported by a following that at times borders on the fanatic. Nevertheless there is pressure, and it is all the greater because it is symptomatic of another need, the need for increasing rationalization. There is a general idea that everything must be based on reason, much as everything must be explained by science. Faith seems to have no clearly defined place, with the result that it is everywhere. In politics, especially, the belief exists that it is possible to base ideological choices on reason. Marcuse chose total emancipation, total liberation. But how did he justify this choice?

Marcuse turned to reason to justify his utopianism, despite the fact that he considered reason a repressive concept.[60] "The free play of thought and imagination," he wrote, "assumes a rational and directing function in the realization of a pacified existence of man and nature."[61] Nevertheless, it is easy to show that utopianism is the result of bad rationalization, as Karl Popper did so effectively.[62] Utopianism has a specific method of reasoning: an action is rational if, and only if, we have an end in view; only the end or goal of an action can tell us whether we are acting rationally. Let us apply this argument to politics: political action is only rational if it pursues an end. For Marcuse, this end could only be the utopia of "pacified existence," in which political action would only be rational in relation to what-ought-to-be, that is, to a *utopian end*. The *historical process* which can lead us to this final state is a secondary consideration. All processes, all means that can put us on the historical path toward realization of ultimate goals are supposedly good, including violence. But in trying to justify everything, one ends by justifying nothing. Utopianism is indeed a very attractive theory, but it is dangerous and pernicious: dangerous, because it can lead us into violence, and pernicious, because it is impossible to determine ultimate goals scientifically.

Incidentally, Marcuse did not try to provide scientific justifications. To resist the pseudo-science of positivism, he stated categorically that "critical theory preserves obstinacy as a genuine quality of philosophical thought."[63] (We might also say "persistence" or "opinionatedness" for the original German *Eigensinn*.) He argued in such a way as to make us believe that any other choice was impossible. By opting for happiness and freedom at the outset, and particularly by refusing to consider the initial choice as multiple in nature, he gave ultimate goals preference over concrete, limited objectives, the latter being relegated to a more or less distant future. He refused to take into account the fact that values have conflicting interests and obey many gods, so to speak, and instead used ultimate goals as a justification in a jumble of truths, experiences, prejudices, appearances, facts, myths, beliefs, and certitudes.

Of course, Marcuse's political justifications were not all negative or polemical, but they might well become so if the realization of concrete objectives were ignored, or if one were not true to one's own cause. Both these reservations applied to Marcuse. In the first place, he was not concerned with concrete objectives. For him, these were details to be agreed on later.[64] He asked us to sign a blank check, more or less. Then again, he described himself as a false friend because he urged that everything must be destroyed and changed while at the same time believing that a good many American universities must be protected as bastions of free and critical thought, and as one of the rare instances where it was possible to realize aims within existing institutions.[65]

But the fact of describing himself as a traitor to the movement in no way eliminated the treason. Indeed, it added to the confusion. This did not deter Marcuse, however, since he rather liked confusion.

I should point out that the confusion meant here is not, strictly speaking, that arising from intellectual error, which could be refuted by logical argument. What we are talking about is ideological confusion, which is essentially dissimulation. Olivier Reboul wrote: "An ideology necessarily dissimulates. Not only must it cover up facts that could be used to refute it, or hide the valid reasons of its adversaries, but also, and above all, it must disguise its own nature. To admit the basis of its ideology would be to destroy itself, as light destroys shadow."[66] In order not to destroy itself, therefore, Marcuse's ideological politics had to assume an extreme position. His ideology had to be all-embracing, *total,* and that is why it took the name of utopia.[67] Ideology itself became a totalitarian system "that ceases to serve politics in order to make politics subservient."[68] There is obviously nothing wrong in trying to uncover and understand all the events that influence politics or are influenced by them. But the attempt to politicize everything ends by completely obscuring politics as an activity in itself. Reality is confused enough without deliberately adding to the confusion, whether by applying a double standard in discussing various circumstances, by using only those facts that support one's own argument, or by systematically ignoring the standard requirements of philosophical thought. And yet this is exactly what Marcuse did.

Jean Marabini, who lived with Marcuse for several weeks some time before his death, reported him as saying, "There are . . . points on which I am in total agreement with Voltaire and Marx: one must fight in order that even one's adversaries may have freedom of expression."[69]

Nevertheless, Marcuse more than once stated the contrary. In answer to a question during the debate on "The Problem of Violence and the Radical Opposition," he said, "We should concentrate energy and time on those strata and groups of which we can assume that they will listen and that they can still think."[70] In a conversation with Richard Kearney, he again distinguished between those with whom it is worth arguing, and those with whom it is better to refrain. "A human being who today still thinks that the world ought not to be changed is below the level of discussion."[71] Similarly he made it clear in Habermas's presence that if someone did not accept the fact that his statements were founded on two immutable value judgments, "there is no room for discussion." He went on to enunciate the two main premises of his thought and work.[72]

Marcuse seemed to apply a double standard when speaking of facts. In the first place, we should take no account of facts that others invoke to support their arguments (by others is meant the enemies of total revolution), because "reality is other and more than that codified in the logic and language of facts," and we need to "break the power of facts over the world."[73] However, when it was a question of the facts on which Marcuse based the defense of one of his major theses on the revolutionary agent, he took a different approach.[74] Why? Because "we can no longer speak of the proletariat as the majority of the population," he told Jean Elleinstein. "We no longer talk of the dictatorship of the proletariat. And the reason is the facts."[75]

Astounding as it may seem, Marcuse held that confusion is a characteristic of philosophical thought. The following is a highly significant anecdote recounted by Robert Paul Wolff, who co-authored *A Critique of Pure Tolerance* with Barrington Moore and Marcuse. The authors were looking for a title agreeable to all. In order to find a common ground, Wolff suggested that it would at least be possible to agree on the desirability of a *clear* title. At this Marcuse lost his temper and stated brusquely that "in philosophy *unclarity* was a virtue"![76]

We all admit that there is confusion in reality. We also must recognize that philosophical thought to some extent reflects this confusion. But reflection, and in particular philosophical reflection, is an attempt to throw some light on this confusion rather than obscure it even further. Philosophical thought that tries to discern the meaning of things and events normally proceeds by two complementary roads. It first establishes an initial relationship between an event and one or several other events, in order to distinguish between them. It then establishes a second relationship between the event in question and events in general. Philosophy thus elaborates meanings, first through their relationship to the parts in order to gain a clear understanding of the specificity of each part, and secondly through their relationship to the whole, in order to arrive at an overall or global understanding. In the first instance, we can speak of a desire for clarification or an awareness of distinctions (clarity); in the second, of a desire to understand everything or an awareness of hidden relationships (depth).[77]

Marcuse almost always took a macro-sociological perspective—in other words, the large view. On this plane the power of his thought inspired a great many radicals. His weakness lay at the level of distinctions. By refusing all formalism, he fell into the major formalistic trap of asserting that all the right is on one's own side, and that everyone else is wrong. Since he could not avoid distinctions (it is impossible to think without distinctions), he was then confined by an "inflexible manichaean cleavage" characteristic of leftism, as Jean Roy has indicated.[78] To the extent that Marcuse and leftists in general have subscribed to this distinction between we and they, the good and the bad, in order to convince others, they have no longer been willing to operate on the level of mere ideological dissimulation, but have used the power of words for linguistic and politico-cultural subversion.

In an article in the *Los Angeles Times* at Marcuse's death, Russell Jacoby rightly pointed out that "Marcuse was not only a subversive; he was subversive to the subversives."[79] Nevertheless, Marcuse himself made a distinction between his status as an intellectual and that of revolutionary activists. "I particularly object to the juxtaposition of my name and photograph with those of Che Guevara, Debray, Rudi Dutschke, etc., because these men have truly risked and are still risking their lives in the battle for a more human society, whereas I participate in this battle only through my words and my ideas. It is a fundamental difference."[80] Marcuse wanted to be, and was, a utopian or romantic revolutionary. And here the confusion resulting from his romanticism almost led him to contradict himself. On one hand, he admitted that a fundamental change was probably possible without violence, particularly in the United States.[81] On the other, he recognized that he was preaching violence in order to achieve a completely pacified society.[82] While he felt somewhat embarassed at passing for a prophet or guru of the New Left, he was proud that his writing was fanning the fires of political confrontation on campuses, in black ghettoes, or in pitched battles with the police. Donald Robinson, in his work on *The 100 Most Important People in the World Today*, correctly identified Marcuse as the one who "firmly supports the violent moves of frenetic activists all over the world."[83] For Marcuse, the important thing was not to implement any particular revolution, but to prepare for revolution in general, or total revolution, "to develop the consciousness that will bring about a revolutionary situation,"[84] to expose everything that impedes the advent of "the impossible revolution," as he called it,[85] and to encourage the hope for qualitative change inherent in the meaning of "a qualitative leap." He was not interested in assuming power, which is the real goal of a revolution, but in the destruction of power, which is the goal of subversion. For him, the revolution took place on the plane of ultimate goals, and subversion was the means to a revolutionary situation rich in all the promises of utopia. There is, therefore, a difference between subversive and revolutionary practice, a difference that Mikel Dufrenne clearly identified in his *Subversion-perversion*.[86] Revolutionary practice inspired by Marxism denounces utopia, whereas subversive practice looks to it as a goal. A century of Marxist revolutionary practice has brought about political change—political change that has become bogged down in bureaucracy and dogma, with the result that today the New Left has fallen into disrepute. Recognizing that political revolution has not produced the new man so eagerly awaited, the subversive practice of the New Left ceased to oppose power in order to oppose society, culture, and the system. As it is impossible to change the entire system through revolution, the system is therefore attacked piecemeal; "but because the system constitutes a totality," explains Mikel Dufrenne, "in order to make inroads at particular points, subversion attacks it as a whole."[87] Subersive practice "operates on a terrain other than politics."[88] It is a utopian practice,[89] a practice aimed at creating the new man right away, and which is connected to what Marcuse calls "the aesthetic-erotic dimension,"[90] or "the moral sexual rebellion."[91] The transformation of individuals, who in turn will be able to transform the system, must take place at the level where the erotic, the aesthetic, and the ethical meet. In the final analysis, subjective factors override objective factors so that there is no real objective means of subversion.

In the end, as with most utopias, it was on the education of individuals that Marcuse counted most. And yet, with typical ambiguity, when he spoke of preferring the dictatorship of intellectuals to that of the proletariat,[92] it was in a spirit of deliberate provocation.[93]

V

Marcuse's Revolutionary Ethics

Like Rousseau, Marcuse believed in the value of negative philosophy. One must know that-which-is-not in order to judge properly that-which-is.[1] The comparison of "that-which-is" to "that-which-is-not" is the basic requirement of a system of ethics that is increasingly critical.[2] Marcuse demonstrated in his 1938 critique "On Hedonism" that from the ancient world through the Christian Middle Ages to the bourgeois period, "The moral interpretation of happiness, its subjection to a universal law of reason, tolerated both the essential isolation of the autonomous person and his actual limitation."[3] However, he himself used morality to condemn present society because, he said, "morality has long ceased to be mere ideology,"[4] and "the humanitarian and moral arguments are not merely deceitful ideology. Rather, they can and must become central social forces."[5] In Marcuse's view, historical conditions changed sufficiently between 1938 and 1967 to justify both the earlier condemnation of traditional morality, and the later recourse to "a certain moral tradition," as in his 1958 comparison of Soviet and Western ethics in *Soviet Marxism*.[6] On one hand there is the tradition of Western society—a tradition that, according to Marcuse, presupposes the possibility of fulfilling the nature of reasonable man within existing institutions. On the other is the heretical tradition to which Soviet and orthodox Marxist ethics belong with respect to their use of the humanist ideals of the Enlightenment, the French Revolution, and German idealism.[7] The problem which Marcuse enunciated was this: what conditions are needed to realize the humanist ideal today? His solution was "libertarian socialism,"[8] which in turn raised other problems. How did Marcuse resolve the question, inherent in any utopia, of the relation between the ethics of conscience and the ethics of responsibility? Why did he resort to a "double morality"? In the final analysis, did his use of the notion of "aesthetic morality" transform his politicism into moralism?

Max Weber's famous distinction between the ethics of conscience and responsibility in his essay, "Politics as a Vocation," is very useful in pinpointing the difficult relation between ethics and politics.[9] Paul Ricoeur employed it in his article, "The Tasks of the Political Educator."[10] Weber's solution to this basic paradox of action is well known. Reasonable action is based both on responsibility, which guides the statesman in justifying his actions, and on conscience, which guides the citizen in his critique of the statesman. These complementary guidelines meet in the reasonable man. Marcuse's solution to this paradox is perhaps less well known. He formulated it by trying to imagine the criticisms that, as he put it, "I hope you have long been addressing to me" for having developed "a utopia in which it is asserted that modern industrial society could soon reach a state in which the principle of repression that has previously directed its development will prove itself obsolete."[11] It was as though he felt a need to clear himself: "It may be less irresponsible today to depict a utopia that has a real basis than to defame as utopia conditions and potentials that have long become realizable possibilities."[12] Utopia, in fact, offers a good example of how the ethics of conscience influence the ethics of responsibility. As Ricoeur explained, it is the historical function of utopia to give economic, social, and political activity a doubly human aim. Humanity should be seen both as a totality guided by a universal ethic, and as a singularity or a unique condition in which the vocation of each individual is realized.[13] This is why a healthy balance must be maintained between the ethics of conscience and responsibility.[14] But in line with the rest of his philosophy, Marcuse subordinated the ethics of responsibility to the ethics of conscience, forgetting that, as Ricoeur pointed out, "A utopian thesis, it is necessary to repeat, does not have an effectiveness of its own; it has such only to the extent that it transforms step by step the historical experience that we are able to make on the level of institutions and on the level of industries. This is why utopia becomes falsehood when it is not articulated correctly concerning the possibilities offered to each epoch."[15] It was these concrete historical facts that Marcuse consciously and deliberately suppressed, for example, during the discussion following his remarks at the 1964 conference on Max Weber at Heidelberg. This passage has already been cited in another context, but bears repeating here: "I would really like to confess to Utopia for the simple reason that nowadays the concept of Utopia has become meaningless. If we look at present-day intellectual and material wealth, if we look at ourselves, what we know and can do, there is actually nothing which rationally and with a good conscience we should despise and denounce as Utopian. We could actually do anything today. We could certainly have a rational society, and just *because* that is such a near possibility its actual realization is more "Utopian" than ever before; the whole force of the *status quo* is mobilized against it."[16]

Basically, he was speaking of himself. Note, however, that he spoke in the conditional, the utopian tense. We can observe, as did Weber, that by adopting the ethics of conscience, Marcuse became a prophet of the millenium.[17] What is more, by setting aside the ethics of responsibility he also postponed the choice of the means suited to the desired end. The only thing he retained was an ideal of perfection supposedly handed down to us through two long and parallel traditions—the heretical or revolutionary tradition, and the orthodox or reactionary tradition. This brings us to the eternal problem of a double moral standard: my ethics are good, yours are bad.

"I believe there is a double moral standard in history," stated Marcuse unequivocally in answer to Julien Freund during the discussion following his lecture on "Freedom and the Historical Imperative." In the lecture he had stated, "There has always been a dual morality: that of the status quo, . . . and revolutionary morality."[18] Marcuse used this dualist approach in judging a situation such as the Watergate scandal. Americans tried to show that it was a case of exceptional corruption, an aberration, he explained, when in fact it was merely "an extreme political form of the normal state of things." Watergate should be seen in context, he maintained, the context being that of American capitalism, which could only perpetuate itself through illegal and illegitimate means—in other words, through the use of violence in the various branches of intellectual and material culture.[19] With Marcuse, as the following statement shows, the theory of a double moral standard corresponded to a double standard of violence. "There is a violence of police forces or armed forces or the Ku Klux Klan, and there is a violence in the opposition to these aggressive manifestations of violence."[20] Elsewhere, he distinguished between "the institutionalized violence of the established system and the violence of resistance."[21] He made a further distinction: "In terms of historical function, there is a difference between revolutionary and reactionary violence, between violence practiced by the oppressed and by the oppressors."[22] Marcuse appeared to see it as a very straightforward matter: two parallel traditions, two kinds of morality, and two types of violence. Yet, in his contribution to *A Critique of Pure Tolerance*, which is a somewhat cavalier mixture of ethics and politics, the terms he used gave a different impression. He appeared to favor the specifically utopian technique of inversion, coining contradictory expressions such as totalitarian democracy, democratic dictatorship, and repressive tolerance. Indeed, he seemed to positively wallow in opposites, although when we look more closely we find that here, too, he distinguished between totalitarian democracy[23] and real democracy,[24] between democratic dictatorship[25] and dictatorship period,[26] and between repressive tolerance and liberating tolerance, which he defined as being "intolerance against movements from the Right, and toleration of movements from the Left."[27]

What was this liberating tolerance that Marcuse advanced as one of the principle values of revolutionary ethics? It was the type of tolerance which *must* be practiced by the revolutionary or intellectual in order to reaffirm the existence of "historical possibilities which seem to have become utopian possibilities."[28] For Marcuse, then, it was a moral duty to proclaim the end of utopia, because "all the material and intellectual forces which could be put to work for the realization of a free society are at hand. That they are not used for that purpose is to be attributed to the total mobilization of existing society against its own potential for liberation."[29]

In other words, as he remarked in *One-Dimensional Man*, "The unrealistic sound of these propositions is indicative, not of their utopian character, but of the strength of the forces which prevent their realization."[30] Contemporary society must not be condemned for what it has accomplished (and it has done more than any other), but for what it refuses to do, by which is meant the total liberation of the individual, the total emancipation of humanity. Marcuse submitted to this revolutionary ideal because he did not consider it possible to progress toward a better society through the historical continuum. There must be a break.[31] "A non-explosive evolution" would produce nothing.[32] Only an authentic revolution could guarantee qualitative change, which was why Marcuse put the following question: "Can a revolution be justified as right, as good, perhaps even as necessary, and justified not merely in political terms . . . but in ethical terms?"[33] Furthermore, "Is the revolutionary use of violence justifiable as a means for establishing or promoting human freedom and happiness?"[34] He tried to prove that the use of violence for radical, qualitative, social change was justified if one applied "ethical terms such as 'right' or 'good' . . . to political . . . movements."[35] In so doing, he confronted us with the distinction between the just and unjust enemy of revolutionary ideology.[36] The just enemy is always revolutionary, while the unjust enemy is always against the revolution. However, the notion of the unjust enemy is based on a confusion between ethics and politics.

Marcuse deliberately maintained this confusion for subversive purposes; the ultimate goals of his liberating project masked the consequences of action. He pretended to be unaware that the implementation of a generous idea could have dangerous consequences, in virtue of what Max Weber called "the paradox of consequences."[37] Marcuse saw the transcendent historical project as a feasible present-day goal, since both technology and economy could now guarantee general emancipation. The project justified the use of revolutionary violence that would end man's domination of man, and inaugurate a reign of happiness. In effect, revolutionary ethics were to guarantee the transition from traditional morality, according to which the personal ideal is impervious to happiness, to a morality that could accommodate an aesthetic ideal. Marcuse stated, "If the individual is ever to come under the power of the ideal to the extent of believing that his concrete longings and needs are to be found in it—found moreover in a state of fulfillment and gratification, then the ideal must give the illusion of granting present satisfaction. It is this illusory reality that neither philosophy nor religion can attain. Only art achieves it—in the medium of beauty."[38]

These revolutionary ethics were transitory. Marcuse claimed that they could bring about a "new morality,"[39] an "aesthetic morality"[40] that would realize both the ethical and aesthetic ideals at once. But here again Marcuse was open to the charge of being misleading. Although it is true that the beautiful and the good resemble each other in several respects, and that beauty can be a "symbol of morality," as is the Kantian expression[41] used by Marcuse,[42] it is no less true that there are differences which Marcuse passed over. Indeed, we might well compare Marcuse's vision, which tended toward a unity of all values, with what Max Weber called "the antagonism of values."[43]

But this is not the only misleading aspect of Marcuse's discourse that I feel should be brought into the open. There is another, and to my way of thinking, more serious aspect. Marcuse, anxious to discover the "common denominator of aesthetics and politics," made use of the idea of an "aesthetic *ethos*."[44] He well understood that the fate of a civilization is decided at this level of values, and he actually proposed a new *ethos* that would assume the role of a universal *ethos*. On the strictly ethical level, this universal *ethos* was the direct opposite of puritanism.[45] On the ethico-religious level, it was the negation of the Judeo-Christian tradition, although only in part, since it needed the revolutionary elements inherent in the promise of happiness and freedom.[46] And finally, looking at the question from the political perspective in the sense that Marcuse understood it—that is, from a unitary, universal perspective—this new aesthetic *ethos* was formulated in accordance with the dual connotation of the word aesthetic.[47] On one hand, it implied a new sensitivity that would create a "libidinal morality"[48] and "*aesthetic* needs."[49] On the other, it related to art, which would include science.[50] According to Marcuse, this was the only valid way, the only permissible *telos* or ultimate end. He underscored this view by noting that it involved "the aesthetic *ethos* of socialism" in which "the construction of the world of art" may be "akin to the reconstruction of the real world."[51] It would not involve just any socialism, however, only that aimed at realizing utopia.[52]

In the last analysis, the ultimate criterion of the Marcusian perspective is the dichotomy between that-which-is and that-which-should-be, between barbarism and socialism, Thanatos and Eros. In discussing the last two basic principles or explanatory hypotheses, he asserted that he would have been unable to comprehend present events, were it not for the concept of the destructive instinct posited in Freud's metapsychology. "Today the intensification of this instinct is a political necessity for those in power. Without this hypothesis I must believe that the world has become crazy and that we are being ruled by madmen, or by criminals or by idiots, and that we have let ourselves go to pieces."[53] As for the constructive instinct that would inspire the building of a non-repressive civilization, he wrote that "today the fight for life, the fight for Eros, is the *political* fight."[54]

Marcuse saw only one solution, in consequence: while awaiting the revolution we must prepare future humanity for a radical change through adequate education. "All education today is therapy: therapy in the sense of liberating man by all available means from a society in which, sooner or later, he is going to be transformed into a brute, even if he doesn't notice it any more. Education in this sense is therapy, and all therapy is political theory and practice."[55] This political education had already begun at the university level,[56] he felt, and must be spread to include all human activities, "all spheres of culture."[57] The more the all-powerful, contemporary technology is dominated by the establishment, "the more it will become dependent on political direction."[58] Instead of being "an instrument of destructive politics,"[59] the established technology could be "a political *a priori*" for "pacified existence."[60] Science must therefore be put to work for social reorganization.[61] Moral argument must become a social force.[62] Art is not meaningful unless it can join in the "political struggle,"[63] for only the aesthetic dimension can guarantee the revolution of the twenty-first century.[64]

Conclusion

Does the hope of modernity lie in Marcuse's utopia? That is the initial question posed by this book. Marcuse tried to convince us that society was one-dimensional. In the past, he explained, there were two dimensions. The social dimension allowed man to integrate himself with society; the personal dimension permitted him to question society. This second dimension no longer exists, he asserted, because the system today assimilates everything. The loss of man's faculty for negative thought has forced him into an impasse. No matter what reforms are made, they reinforce rather than change the system. Only revolution is left, but even that is impossible because the forces opposing it are too powerful, despite the fact that general economic and technological conditions have never been so promising, and that the suppression of utopia through its realization has become a genuine possibility. But, we may ask, is existing society in fact moving toward the suppression of utopia, comparable to Marx's suppression of philosophy? In reality, specific human activities continue to be numerous. Politics, for example, has its particular phenomena, such as the police and the army; religion has its own special manifestations, such as prayer and mystical theology. One cannot resolve political or economic problems with ethics, or vice versa. It is impossible to reduce all human activities to a single entity—even if it were art. And the fact that there are many activities means that there are many values. Each activity creates its own values, which do not necessarily harmonize with the values of others. It is therefore not logically justifiable to propose a transcendent historical project to humankind solely because it is founded on values such as freedom and happiness. Marcuse relied on the assumption that man would have the option of choosing so grandiose a project. But if man still has the possibility of choice, it is because he has not yet been totally alienated by his past. In any case, if he makes a definitive choice such as Marcuse proposed, particularly without knowing exactly where it will lead, he is surely alienating himself with regard to his future. This is the underlying significance of Marcuse's utopia: it closes humanity in upon itself, as utopia confines itself within its insular perspective. But let us immediately add that Marcuse, more than anyone else, was aware of the problem of encirclement. Indeed, the dilemma of the vicious circle was one of the things for which he became known. And this is probably why he wanted his theory to be understood as a call, a cry of mingled hope and despair. The following anecdote reported by Reinhard Lettau can perhaps help us comprehend his desire.[1] Marcuse recounted how one day someone asked Beckett to explain the structure of his writing. Beckett answered, "I was once in a hospital, and in the room next door a woman who was dying of cancer screamed all night. This screaming is the structure of my writing."

Marcuse has made this terminal cry his own, describing it with Wedekind's words from the last scene of *Pandora's Box*: "Es war doch so schön!"—"So fair has it been!"[2] And he echoes Strindberg's cry from *Dreamplay*: "Es ist schade um di Menschen"—"It is a pity about human beings!"[3]

Notes

Abbreviations of Works by Marcuse

AC *Actuels*. Paris: Editions Galilée, 1976.

AD *The Aesthetic Dimension: Toward a Critique of Marxist Aesthetics*. Boston: Beacon Press, 1978.

CRR *Counterrevolution and Revolt*. Boston: Beacon Press, *1972*.

EC *Eros and Civilization: A Philosophical Inquiry into Freud*. Boston: Beacon Press, 1955.

EL *An Essay on Liberation*. Boston: Beacon Press, 1969.

FL *Five Lectures: Psychoanalysis, Politics, and Utopia*. Boston: Beacon Press, 1970.

FU *La Fin de l'utopie*. Paris: Seuil, et Neuchâtel: Delachaux et Niestlé, 1968.

HU *L'Homme unidimensionnel, Essai sur l'idéologie de la société industrielle avancée*. Paris: Editions de Minuit, [1964] 1968.

NE *Negations: Essays in Critical Theory*. Boston: Beacon Press, 1969.

ODM *One-Dimensional Man: Studies in the Ideology of Advanced Industrial Society*. Boston: Beacon Press, 1964.

RR *Reason and Revolution: Hegel and the Rise of Social Theory*. Boston: Beacon Press [1941] 1960.

RT "Repressive Tolerance." In *A Critique of Pure Tolerance*. Boston: Beacon Press, 1965.

SCP *Studies in Critical Philosophy*. Boston: Beacon Press, 1972.

SM *Soviet Marxism: A Critical Analysis*. New York: Random House, Vintage Books [1958] 1961.

Introduction

1. Alexandre Cioranescu, *L'Avenir du passé* (Paris: Gallimard, 1972), 121.

2. Karl Marx, "Contribution to the Critique of Hegel's Philosophy of Law, Introduction," *Karl Marx, Frederick Engels: Collected Works*, (New

York: International Publishers, 1975), 3:187. Subsequent references to Marx and Engels are to this edition, unless otherwise stated.

3. Henri Lefebvre, *Pour connaître la pensée de Karl Marx* (Paris: Bordas, [1947] 1966), 100.

4. "Philosophy and Critical Theory," in *NE*, 151-152. Cited by Gérard Raulet, "Pour une reconstruction de la théorie critique: L'Intégration des valeurs de la critique," in Paul-Laurent Assoun and Gérard Raulet, *Marxisme et théorie critique* (Paris: Payot, 1978), 124.

5. Ibid., 153.

6. Karl Marx, "Theses on Feuerbach," *Karl Marx, Frederick Engels: Collected Works*, 5:5.

7. "Préface" (1964), *Culture et société* (Paris: Editions de Minuit, 1970), 18. Cf., *NE*, xx.

8. *NE*, xix.

9. *EL*, ix.

10. *SM*, 5.

11. Herbert Marcuse, *Eros et civilisation* (Paris: Editions de Minuit, 1968), 10 (from a special preface written in 1961 for the French edition). Cf., *EC*, 5.

12. See *ODM*, 4, and "The End of Utopia," in *FL*, 64, 65.

13. Herbert Marcuse, "Liberation from the Affluent Society," in *To Free a Generation: The Dialectics of Liberation*, ed. David Cooper (Harmondsworth: Penguin Books Ltd., 1969), 184.

14. Herbert Marcuse, "Protosocialism and Late Capitalism: Toward a Theoretical Synthesis Based on Bahro's Analysis," *International Journal of Politics* 10, nos. 2-3 (Summer-Fall 1980): 25, 33; this essay also published in *Rudolf Bahro: Critical Responses*, ed. Ulf Wolter (White Plains, N.Y.: M.E. Sharpe, Inc., 1980), 25-48. See also id., "Sommes-nous déjà des hommes?" *Partisans* 28 (April 1966): 26; "On the New Left," in *The New Left: A Documentary History*, ed. Massimo Teodori (Indianapolis: Bobbs-Merrill, 1969), 469; and "Liberation from the Affluent Society," 184.

15. "The End of Utopia," *FL*, 63.

16. "Philosophy and Critical Theory," *NE*, 143.

17. Leszek Kolakowski, *L'Esprit révolutionnaire suivi de Marxisme: Utopie et anti-utopie* (Brussels: Editions Complexe, 1978), 113.

18. Sidney Lipshires, *Herbert Marcuse: From Marx to Freud and Beyond*, (Cambridge: Schenkman Publishing Co., 1974).

19. Morton Schoolman, *The Imaginary Witness: The Critical Theory of Herbert Marcuse* (New York: Free Press, 1980).

20. Vincent Geoghegan, *Reason and Eros: The Social Theory of Herbert Marcuse* (London: Pluto Press, 1981).

21. Martin Jay, *The Dialectical Imagination: A History of the Frankfurt School and the Institute of Social Research, 1923-1950* (London: Heinemann, 1973).

22. David Held, *Introduction to Critical Theory: Horkheimer to Habermas* (Berkeley: University of California Press, 1980).
23. George Friedman, *The Political Philosophy of the Frankfurt School* (Ithaca and London: Cornell University Press, 1981).
24. Gérard Raulet, "Pour une reconstruction de la théorie critique," 101-148.
25. Ben Agger, *Western Marxism: An Introduction, Classical and Contemporary Sources* (Santa-Monica: Goodyear Publishing, 1979).
26. Thomas Molnar, *Utopia, the Perennial Heresy* (New York: Sheed and Ward, 1967), 234-235, 205.
27. Jean-Marie Domenach, "Utopie ou la raison dans l'imaginaire," *Esprit* (April 1974): 351, n. 11.

Chapter I

1. Herbert Marcuse, "On the Question of Reform or Revolution," *Listening*, 8, nos. 1-2-3 (1973): 88.
2. Erica Sherover Marcuse and Peter Marcuse, "Open Letter to Friends of Herbert Marcuse," *New German Critique*, 6, no. 3: 28.
3. Gershom Scholem, *Fidélité et utopie: Essais sur le judäisme contemporain*, (Paris: Calmann-Lévy, 1978), 256.
4. Herbert Marcuse, "Révolution et critique de la violence: Sur la philosophie de l'histoire de Walter Benjamin," *Revue d'esthétique*, no. 1 (1981): 101-102. Cf., Walter Benjamin, "Nachwort," *Zur Kritik der Gewalt und andere Aufsatze* (Frankfurt am Main: Suhrkamp Verlag, 1965), 99-106. On Judaism in the Frankfurt School, see George Friedman, *The Political Philosophy of the Frankfurt School* (Ithaca: Cornell University Press), 92-102.
5. "Can Communism Be Liberal?" *New Statesman*, 83, no. 2153 (23 June 1972): 861. Aron: "You are still living in Weimar Germany." Marcuse: "Yes I know that."
6. *FL*, 102-103.
7. "Theory and Politics: A Discussion with Herbert Marcuse, Jürgen Habermas, Heinz Lubasz, and Telman Spengler," trans. by Leslie Adelson, Susan Hegger, Betty Sun, and Herbert Weinryb, *Telos*, 11, no. 3 (Winter 1978-79): 126. Italics mine.
8. Jóhann Páll Arnason, "Marcuse critique de stalinisme," *Partisans*, no. 68 (Nov.-Dec. 1972): 103.
9. "Révolution et critique de la violence," 105.
10. Claude Samuel, "La Faute à Marcuse . . . ," *Le Point*, no. 256 (17 Oct. 1977): 88.
11. "Dear Angela," *Ramparts Magazine*, 9 (Feb. 1971): 22.
12. Marcuse, "Protosocialism and Late Capitalism."
13. Marcuse summed up the protest of the sixties in a little-known special interview with the director of the collection "Les Grands Thèmes"

(GT). Henri Tissot, ed., *Les Jeunes et la contestation*, vol. 93 of *Bibliothèque Laffont des grands thèmes* (Lausanne: Editions Grammont; Paris: Robert Laffont; and Barcelona: Salvat, 1975), 8-17, 60-67.

14. Douglas Kellner, "In Remembrance of Herbert Marcuse, 1898-1979," *Socialist Review*, 9, no. 5 (Sept.-Oct. 1979): 133.

15. Ivo Franzel, "Utopia and Apocalypse in German Literature," *Social Research*, 39, no. 2 (Summer 1972): 307. (This was a special number devoted to the Weimar culture.)

16. Cf., Philippe Beneton, *Histoire de mots: Culture et civilisation* (Paris: Presses de la Fondation nationale des sciences politiques, 1975).

17. "The Revolution Never Came," *Time Magazine*, Canadian ed., 13 Aug. 1979, 13.

18. "On the Question of Reform or Revolution," 88.

19. Jay, *The Dialectical Imagination*, 28.

20. Jean-Michel Palmier, "Le Groupe de novembre ou l'art comme arme révolutionnaire," in *Apocalypse et révolution*, vol. 1 of *L'Expressionnisme comme révolte, Contribution à l'étude de la vie artistique sous la République de Weimar* (Paris: Payot, 1978), 392-400.

21. Jay, *The Dialectical Imagination*, 28.

22. "On the Question of Reform or Revolution," 89.

23. "Theory and Politics," 126.

24. Jay, *The Dialectical Imagination*, 8.

25. Sidney Lipshires, *Herbert Marcuse: From Marx to Freud and Beyond* (Cambridge: Schenkman Publishing Co., 1974), 13 n. 43.

26. Cf., Jürgen Habermas, "Psychic Thermidor and the Rebirth of Rebellious Subjectivity," *Berkeley Journal of Sociology*, 24-25 (1980): 6. See also Kellner, "In Remembrance of Herbert Marcuse," 132.

27. On the Frankfurt School see: Andrew Arato, "Political Sociology and Critique of Politics," in *The Essential Frankfurt School Reader*, eds. Andrew Arato and Eike Gebhardt (New York,: Urizen Books, 1978) 3-25; *Esprit*, special issue on the Frankfurt School, no. 17 (May 1979); David Held, *Introduction to Critical Theory, Horkheimer to Habermas*, selective bibliography 483-499, index 501-511, and passim; Richard Kilminster, *Praxis and Method: A Sociological Dialogue with Lukács, Gramsci and the Early Frankfurt School* (London, Henley, and Boston: Routledge & Kegan Paul, 1979), cf., index 329; Leszek Kolakowski, "The Frankfurt School and 'Critical Theory,' " translated by P.S. Falla, in *The Breakdown*, vol. 3 of *Main Currents of Marxism, Its Origin, Growth, and Dissolution* (Oxford: Clarendon Press, 1978) 341-395, esp. 344-345, 348, 377, 390; Phil Slater, *Origin and Significance of the Frankfurt School: A Marxist Perspective* (London: Routledge & Kegan Paul, 1977), index 183-185.

28. Paul A. Robinson, *The Freudian Left* (New York: Harper and Row, 1969), 151, citing *International Institute of Social Research: A Report on Its History, Aims, and Activities, 1933-1938*, 4, 6.

29. David Held, *Introduction to Critical Theory*, 14-15.
30. Jay, *The Dialectical Imagination*, 39.
31. Karl Marx, "Le Projet d'émigration du citoyen Cabet," *La Revue communiste*, no. 1 (1958), cited by Louis Marin, *Utopiques: Jeux d'espaces*, (Paris: Les Editions de Minuit, 1973), 343-351.
32. "Preface to the Original Edition," *RR* (pocket edition), xv.
33. "Theory and Politics," 129.
34. Max Horkheimer, "Traditional and Critical Theory," (1937), *Critical Theory*, translated by J.O. Matthew, Connell, et al., (1937; New York: The Seabury Press, 1972), 188-252.
35. Ibid., 244.
36. Ibid., 244-252.
37. *NE*, 134-158.
38. Martin Jay attributes the first use of the expression "critical theory" to Max Horkheimer. "The Frankfurt School in Exile," in *Perspectives in American History*, 6:340. Therefore texts written before the year 1937 merely contain expressions that prefigure what subsequently became the "critical theory" of the Frankfurt School. Thus, in Marcuse's first published article in 1928, we find him using expressions such as "theory of social activity," or "theory of historical action" to describe what he understood by Marxism at that time. (Cf., "Contributions to a Phenomenology of Historical Materialism.") What distinguishes these expressions from "critical theory" is the desire to make a contribution to Marxist thought.
39. William Leiss, "The Critical Theory of Society: Present Situation and Future Tasks," in *Critical Interruptions: New Left Perspectives on Herbert Marcuse*, ed. Paul Breines, (New York: Herder and Herder, 1970), 75.
40. Ibid., 76, 88-89.
41. "Theory and Politics," 136. See also *NE*, 15, 135.
42. *ODM*, x-xi.
43. Cf., Horkheimer, "Traditional and Critical Theory," 244 n.1.
44. Ibid., 242.
45. Kellner, "In Remembrance of Herbert Marcuse," 132.
46. Jay, *The Dialectical Imagination*, 80.
47. "On the Question of Reform or Revolution," 89.
48. Charles Moritz, ed., *Current Biography Yearbook, 1969*, 283. See also Jay, *The Dialectical Imagination*, 169.
49. Sidney Lipshires, *Herbert Marcuse: From Marx to Freud and Beyond*, 27.
50. *EC*, xxviii.
51. John Wakeman, ed., *World Authors, 1950-1970*, 945.
52. "Acknowledgments," *SM*, xvii.
53. Jóhann Páll Arnason, "Marcuse critique du stalinisme," *Partisans*, no. 68 (Nov.-Dec. 1972): 103.
54. "On the Question of Reform or Revolution," 90.

55. Andrew Hacker, "Philosopher of the New Left," *The New York Times Book Review*, 73, no. 10 (10 Mar. 1968): 1.
56. Habermas, "Psychic Thermidor and the Rebirth of Rebellious Subjectivity," 9.
57. *Who's Who in America with World Notables*, 35 (1968-69).
58. Habermas, "Psychic Thermidor," 2.
59. *ODM*, xvi.
60. Robert Paul Wolff, "Herbert Marcuse: 1898-1979, A Personal Reminiscence," *Political Theory*, 8, no. 1 (Feb. 1980): 7.
61. "Industrialization and Capitalism in the Work of Max Weber," *NE*, 201-226.
62. Benjamin Nelson, "Storm over Weber," *The New York Times Book Review*, 3 Jan. 1965, sec. 7, p. 24.
63. Raymond Aron, *Les Etapes de la pensée sociologique* (Paris: Gallimard), 566.
64. "Comment," *The New York Times Book Review*, 28 Feb. 1965.
65. "Industrialisation et capitalisme chez Max Weber," *CS*, 273. Note the difference between this and the last paragraph in the English published version.
66. *NE*, 203.
67. Michael Horowitz, "Portrait of the Marxist as an Old Trouper," *Playboy*, 17, no. 9 (1970): 175-176, 228, 231-232.
68. Ibid., 176, citing Marcuse.
69. *NE*, xx.
70. *ODM*, 4.
71. Melvin J. Lasky, "Lettre de Berlin-Ouest, avec les étudiants du S.D.S.," *Preuves*, nos. 215-216 (Feb.-Mar. 1969), 68. See also commentary by Jacques Ellul, *De la révolution aux révoltes* (Paris: Calmann-Lévy, 1972), 300 n. 2.
72. *The Times*, London, 17 Apr. 1968, p. 10.
73. "Interview with Marcuse," *Australian Left Review* (Dec. 1969): 36.
74. Ibid., 38-39.
75. André François-Poncet, "La Crise de la jeunesse allemande," *Le Figaro, Sélection hebdomadaire*, 18 Apr. 1968.
76. "Menaces de mort," *Le Figaro*, 5 Aug. 1968.
77. Gladwin Hill, "The Marcuse Case: Conservatism Aroused by a Legionnaire in San Diego," *The New York Times*, 6 Oct. 1968, sec. 1, 86.
78. *The Times*, London, 19 Feb. 1969, 6.
79. Ibid., 12 July 1968, 6.
80. Herbert Gold, "California Left, Mao, Marx and Marcuse!" *The Saturday Evening Post*, no. 241 (27 Oct. 1968): 57.
81. Ibid., 56-59.
82. Edmund Stillman, "Herbert Marcuse," *Horizon*, 11, no. 3 (Summer 1969) 27.

83. Agnès Guillou, "Marcuse pour quoi faire?" *La Nef*, no. 36 (Jan.-Mar. 1969): 7.

84. "*New Left News*, the irregular newsletter of the Columbia University SDS, offers an *Adventures of One-Dimensional Man* comic strip." Paul Breines, "Marcuse and the New Left in America," in *Antworten auf Herbert Marcuse*, ed. Jürgen Habermas (Frankfurt am Main: Suhrkamp, 1968), 141.

85. Charlotte Delbo, *La Théorie et la pratique, Dialogue imaginaire mais non tout à fait apocryphe entre H. Marcuse et H. Lefebvre* (Paris: Editions Anthropos, 1969).

86. Peter Clecak, *Radical Paradoxes* (New York: Harper & Row, 1973), 212.

87. Wolff, "Herbert Marcuse: A Personal Reminiscence," 7.

88. Gérard Bergeron, "Qui est Herbert Marcuse?" *L'Enseignement*, no. 8, (15 Dec. 1968): 22: "In Italy, two films are being shot. *A Mother's Heart* by Salvator Sampieri tells the story of a middle class woman who, on the basis of what she thinks she understands of Marcuse's books, decides to form a gang of young terrorists. The satire is even more exaggerated in Bruno Barrati's film. So that no one can mistake his meaning, he is calling it *The Marcusienne, or the One-Dimensional Woman*. Instead of a modest middle-class woman, he has a millionairess who decides to amuse herself by playing at revolution!"

89. Jean-Michel Palmier, "Portrait d'Herbert Marcuse," in *AC*, 96.

90. Mme N. B., "M. François Perroux introduit Marcuse au Collège de France," *Le Monde*, 29 January 1969, p. 11.

91. François Perroux, *François Perroux interroge Herbert Marcuse. . . qui répond* (Paris: Aubier-Montaigne, 1969), 100.

92. Louis Wiznitzer, "Interview exclusive d'Herbert Marcuse, théoricien révolutionnaire fort doux," *La Presse*, Montreal, 4 Jan. 1969, 7.

93. "U.S. Student Gaoled for Arson Attempt," *The Times*, London, 22 Feb. 1969, 5.

94. Jay Acton, "Mug Shots, Who's Who in the New Earth," *World 1972*, 138.

95. "Pontiff Assails Eroticism Again, Scores Freud and Marcuse in Homily Basilica," *The New York Times*, 2 Oct. 1969, 23.

96. Horowitz, "Portrait of the Marxist as an Old Trouper," 228.

97. Ibid., 231.

98. Allen R. Newman, "Notes on Marcuse's Critique of Industrial Society," *Review of Social Economy*, 34, no. 2 (Oct. 1976): 173.

99. *Britannica Book of the Year*, 1969: 158.

100. Sol Stern, "The Metaphysics of Rebellion," *Ramparts Magazine*, 6 (29 June 1968): 56.

101. Palmier, "Portrait d'Herbert Marcuse," 103.

102. Martin Jay, "The Frankfurt School in Exile," *Perspectives in American History* (Cambridge, Mass.: 1972), 6:382. Others included Ron

Aronson, Michael Horowitz, David Kettler, Donald Lee, Myriam Miedzian Malinovich, and John O'Neill.

103. William Leiss, John David Ober, and Erica Sherover, "Marcuse as Teacher," in *The Critical Spirit, Essays in Honor of Herbert Marcuse*, eds. Kurt H. Wolff and Barrington Moore, Jr., (Boston: Beacon Press, 1967), 421-425.

104. Ibid., 425. Italics mine.

105. Ibid., 424. Italics mine.

106. Raymond Aron, *La Révolution introuvable: Réflexions sur les événements de mai* (Paris: Fayard, 1968), 119.

107. "Professors, One-Dimensional Philosopher," *Time Magazine*, 22 Mar. 1969, 67.

108. "Democracy Has, Hasn't a Future . . . a Present," *The New York Times Magazine*, 26 May 1969, 114. This is a record of a public debate held in New York at a meeting of The Theater for Ideas. Marcuse said, "I now finally reveal myself as a fink."

109. See also Jean Wetz, "Un Désaveu de Böll et Marcuse," *Le Devoir*, Montreal, 20 Sept. 1977, and George Eckstein, "Coping with Terrorism," *Dissent* (Winter 1978): 82-84.

110. Rudi Dutschke, article in *Die Zeit*, 39 (23 Sept. 1977), translated as "Toward Clarifying Criticism of Terrorism," *New German Critique*, 4, no. 3: 9-10.

111. Herbert Marcuse, "Mord darf keine Waffen der Politik sein," *Die Zeit*, 39 (23 Sept. 1977), translated as "Murder is not a Political Weapon," *New German Critique*, 4, no. 3: 7-8.

112. Ibid., 8.

113. Cf., Jeffrey Herf, "The Critical Spirit of Herbert Marcuse," *New German Critique*, 6, no. 3: 24-27.

114. On Freudian Marxism, see "When Dogma Bites Dogma: Or the Difficult Marriage of Marx and Freud," *Times Literary Supplement*, 8 Jan. 1971, 25-27; Ernest Jones, "Sociology," in *Last Years (1919-1939)*, vol. 3 of *The Life and Work of Sigmund Freud* (New York: Basic Books, Inc., 1969); and *Freudo-Marxisme et sociologie de l'aliénation* (Paris: Editions Anthropos and Union générale d'éditions, 1974).

115. Cf., Wilhelm Reich, *La Crise sexuelle*, followed by "Matérialisme dialectique et psychanalyse," a translation expurgated by the French Communist Party (Paris: Editions Sociales Internationales, 1934).

116. Cf., for example, Jacques Mousseau, "Wilhelm Reich précurseur de Marcuse," in *Psychologie*, 9 (Oct. 1970): 10-12, 14-15.

117. Cf., André Nicolas, *Herbert Marcuse ou la quête d'un univers transprométhéen* (Paris: Seghers, 1970), and *Wilhelm Reich ou la révolution radicale* (Paris: Seghers, 1973).

118. Jay, *The Dialectical Imagination*, 89, 98, 100-101, and 104-105.

119. Erich Fromm, *The Revolution of Hope: Toward a Humanized Technology* (New York, Evanston, and London: Harper and Row, 1968), 9.

120. François Châtelet and Gilles Lapouge, "Actualité de l'utopie," in *Quelle crise? Quelle société?* (Grenoble: Presses universitaires de Grenoble, 1974), 33.
121. André Nicolas, *Herbert Marcuse* (Paris: Seghers, 1970), 7.
122. Ibid., p. 13.
123. Gerhard Höhn and Gérard Raulet, "L'Ecole de Francfort en France, Bibliographie critique," *Esprit*, no. 17 (May 1978): 135-147.
124. André Clair, "Une Philosophie de la nature," *Esprit*, no. 377 (Jan. 1969): 68-73.
125. Jean-Marie Vincent, *La Théorie de l'école de Francfort* (Paris: Galilée, 1976), 9.
126. Paul-Laurent Assoun and Gérard Raulet, *Marxisme et théorie critique* (Paris: Payot, 1978).
127. André Stéphane (pseudonum of two psychoanalysts), "Marcuse, contribution à Freud ou contribution aux mythes?" followed by "Marcuse, Massacre pour des bagatelles," in *L"Univers contestationnaire ou les nouveaux chrétiens, Etude psychanalytique* (Paris: Payot, 1969), 169-192 and 193-201.
128. Jules Monnerot, *Sociologie de la révolution, Mythologies politiques du XXe siècle, Marxistes-léninistes et fascistes, La Nouvelle Stratégie révolutionnaire* (Paris: Fayard, 1969), 706.
129. Raymond Ruyer, *Eloge de la société de consommation* (Paris: Calmann-Lévy, 1969), 188.
130. Jacques Ellul, *De la révolution aux révoltes*, 306.
131. Julien Freund, "La Détresse du politique," *Res Publica*, 14, no. 3 (1972): 433.
132. Pierre Masset, *La Pensée de Herbert Marcuse* (Toulouse: Privat, 1969), 188.
133. André Vachet, "Marcuse vu par F. Perroux," *Dialogue*, 9, no. 3 (1970), 425.
134. Perroux, *François Perroux interroge Herbert Marcuse*, 103.
135. René Vienet, *Enragés et Situationnistes dans le mouvement des occupations* (Paris: Gallimard, 1968), 153.
136. Vadim Delaunay, "Marcuse," *Esprit*, no. 9 (Sept. 1977): 20.
137. I. A. Zamoshkin and N. V. Motroshilova, "Is Marcuse's 'Critical Theory of Society' Critical?" *The Soviet Review*, 1, no. 1 (Spring 1970): 3-24.
138. Yury Zhukov, "Taking Marcuse from the Woodshed," *Atlas*, 6, no. 3 (Sept. 1968): 33-35.
139. Alasdair MacIntyre, *Marcuse* (London: Fontana, 1970), 17.
140. Ibid., 92.
141. Lipshires, *From Marx to Freud and Beyond*, 104.
142. Gerd-Klaus Kaltenbrunner, "Mutmassungen über Marcuse," *Neues Forum: Oesterreichische monatblaetter für Kulturelle Freiheit*, 15, Vienna, nos. 169-170 (January 1968): 55-61, and Maria Szecsi, "Zur

Pathologie der Utopie," *Neues Forum*, 15, no. 173 (May 1968): 325-328.

143. Olga Semyonova, "The New Dissidents, Leningrad's Young Intellectuals May Turn to Terrorism," *New Statesman*, 14 Sept. 1979, 374-328.

144. Russian publications on Marcuse are generally reviewed by Thomas J. Blakeley in *Studies in Soviet Thought*.

Chapter II

1. Jean-Michel Palmier, *Herbert Marcuse et la Nouvelle Gauche* (Paris: Belfond, 1973), 378.

2. Henri Desroche, "Petite Bibliothèque de l'Utopie," *Esprit*, no. 434 (Apr. 1974): 663-670).

3. Cioranescu, "L'Avenir du passé," 17.

4. Cf., Frank E. Manuel and Fritzie P. Manuel, *Utopian Thought in the Western World*, 3d ed. (Cambridge, Mass: The Belknap Press of Harvard University Press, 1982). Paul Ricoeur, "Ideology and Utopia as Cultural Imagination," *Philosophic Exchange*, no. 2 (Summer 1976): 17-28, cf., 24-28. This article was completed in the French edition: "L'Herméneutique de la sécularisation, foi, idéologie et utopie," in *Herméneutique de la sécularisation*, Enrico Castelli et al. (Paris: Aubier-Montaigne, 1976), 49-68. Lyman Tower Sargent, "A Note on the Other Side of Human Nature in the Utopian Novel," *Political Theory*, 3, no. 1 (Feb. 1975): 88-97, and "Utopia—The Problem of Definition," *Extrapolation, 16 (May 1975): 137-148. Paul A. Swada, "Toward the Definition of Utopia," in Moreana*, nos. 31-32 (1971): 135-146.

5. *SCP*, 203.

6. "Can Communism Be Liberal?" 861.

7. *EL*, 3-4.

8. *FL*, 62.

9. C. Mossé, "Les Utopies égalitaires à l'époque hellénistique," *Revue historique*, 241 (1969): 297-308.

10. Cioranescu, "L'Avenir du passé," 71.

11. Plato, *Republic*, 472d, 473a, in *The Dialogues of Plato*, translated by B. Jowett, 4th ed. (Oxford: Clarendon Press, 1953), 2:163-499. References to *Republic* and *Laws* are to this edition.

12. Ernst Bloch, *Le Principe Espérance*, translated by Françoise Wuilmart (Paris: Gallimard, 1976) 1:124. Originally published as *Das Prinzip Hoffnung* (Frankfurt am Main: Suhrkamp Verlag, 1959).

13. On the use of the notion of the "day-dream" by Plato and Aristotle, cf., Henri Desroche, *Sociologie de l'espérance* (Paris: Calmann-Lévy, 1973), 23 n. 8.

14. Henri-Irénée Marrou, *Histoire de l'éducation dans l'antiquité* (Paris: Seuil, 1965), cf., 154.

15. Henri Desroche, "L'Origine utopique," *Esprit* (Oct. 1974): 337-366.

16. Paul Ricoeur, E. R. Dodds, and Jean Roy have also formulated the problem in these terms. Paul Ricoeur, "L'Herméneutique de la sécularisation," 58; E. R. Dodds, *Les Grecs et l'irrationnel* (Aubier, 1965); and Jean Roy, "Modernité et utopie," *Philosophiques*, 6, no. 1 (Apr. 1979): 22. Roy cites Dodds' article.

17. Raymond Trousson, *Voyages aux pays de nulle part, Histoire littéraire de la pensée utopique* (Brussels: Editions de l'Université de Bruxelles, 1975), 38.

18. Marrou, "Histoire de l'éducation dans l'antiquité," 116-117.

19. Raymond Ruyer, *L'Utopie et les utopies* (Paris: PUF, 1950), 38.

20. Ibid., 44.

21. Plato, *Republic*, 541a.

22. Molnar, *Utopia, The Perennial Heresy*, 149.

23. Plato, *The Statesman*, 293d-e. This and subsequent citations to *The Statesman* are taken from *Plato:* The Sophist *and* The Statesman, translated by A. E. Taylor (London: Thomas Nelson and Sons Ltd., 1961), 253-344.

24. Molnar, *Utopia, The Perennial Heresy*, 149.

25. Julien Freund, "Anarchie führt zu Diktatur—Was von Herbert Marcuses Philosophie übrig geblieben ist?" *Die Politische Meinung*, no. 148 (May-June 1973): 22-23. In confirmation of Freund's remarks, see *RR*, 394; *EC*, 225; *ODM*, 40; *ER*, 137-138; *RT*, 106, 120-122.

26. *RT*, 106.

27. *RT*, 120.

28. *RT*, 122.

29. "Can Communism Be Liberal?" 861. See also M. J. Sobran, "The Future Future of Marcuse," *National Review*, 8 Dec. 1972, 1352.

30. Ibid.

31. Plato, *The Statesman*, 293d; Jean Jacques Rousseau, "Dernière Réponse de J.-J. Rousseau (à Bordes)," in *Oeuvres complètes*, Bibliothèque de la Pléiade, 3:90-91.

32. Ljubomir Tadić, "Révolution socialiste et pouvoir politique," *Praxis*, nos. 1-2 (1969): 250-259.

33. *FU*, 101.

34. Cf., *RT*, and "Ethics and Revolution," in *Ethics and Society: Original Essays on Contemporary Moral Problems*, ed. Richard T. De George (New York: Doubleday, 1966), 133-147, particularly 137-138.

35. *EC*, 225.

36. "Theory and Politics," 136.

37. Jean Roy, "La 'Tolérance répressive,' nouvelle ruse de la Raison d'Etat?" in *Rationality Today, La Rationalité aujourd'hui*, ed. Theodore F. Geraets (Ottawa: Editions de l'Université d'Ottawa, 1979), 485ff.

38. David Spitz, "Pure Tolerance: A Critique of Criticisms," *Dissent*, 13, no. 5 (Sept.-Oct. 1966): 510-525, reprinted (Spring 1974): 259-269. The article was again reprinted, with an introduction, in *Beyond the New Left*, ed. Irving Howe (New York: McCall Pub. Co., 1970), 100-119. The article was the subject of several commentaries, to which the author replied: (1) Michael Walzer, "On the Nature of Freedom," in *Dissent*, 13, no. 6 (Nov.-Dec. 1966): 725-728; David Spitz, "The Pleasures of Misunderstanding Freedom," ibid., 729-739; (2) Robert Paul Wolff, "On Tolerance and Freedom," in *Dissent*, 14, no. 1 (Jan.-Feb. 1967): 95-97; David Spitz, "A Rejoinder to Robert Paul Wolff," ibid., 97-98; (3) Philip Green, "Again: Tolerance, Democracy, Pluralism, 1. Comment Philip Green," in *Dissent*, 14, no. 3 (May-June 1967): 368-371; David Spitz, "2. A Rejoinder to Philip Green," ibid., 371-372; Philip Green, "3. Philip Green Answers David Spitz," ibid, 372-373.

39. Trousson, *Voyages aux pays de nulle part*, 178.

40. Ruyer, *L'Utopie et les utopies*, 9. On the contradiction in Ruyer's work regarding his distinction between the "utopian mode" and the "utopian genre," cf., Cioranescu, *L'Avenir du passé*, 264-267.

41. Ibid., 187.

42. *RR*, 186.

43. Cf., *RR*, 32, 394; *EC*, 225; *ODM*, 39-40; *SCP*, 98, 112, 122.

44. Freund, "Anarchie fürht zu Diktatur," 21-22. Cf., id., "La Philosophie 'politiciste' de Herbert Marcuse," in *Revue d'Allemagne*, 1 (April-June 1969): 199, 207, and *Utopie et violence* (Paris: Editions Marcel Rivière et Cie., 1978), 116.

45. J.-M. Benoist, "Marcuse, un Aufklärer contre les lumières," in *Marx est mort* (Paris: Gallimard, 1970) 109, 113-127.

46. A. Birou, "Signification du développement des idéologies," *Ecologie et humanisme*, no. 194 (July-Aug. 1970): 9-10.

47. Jean Jacques Rousseau,"Lettres écrites de la montagne," in *Oeuvres complètes*, 3:810; cited by B. Baczko, "Lumières et Utopie," 358-359, with reference to J. Fabre, "Réalité et Utopie dans la pensée politique de J.-J. Rousseau," *Annales J.-J. Rousseau*, 35 (1959-1962): 181-216.

48. Herbert Marcuse, "Sommes-nous déjà des hommes?" *Partisans*, no. 28 (Apr. 1966): 26.

49. Jean Jacques Rousseau, *The Social Contract*, bk. 1, chap. 6. This and subsequent references are taken from Jean Jacques Rousseau, *The Social Contract: An Eighteenth-Century Translation Completely Revised, Edited, with an Introduction*, ed. Charles Frankel (New York: Hafner Publishing Co., 1947).

50. *ODM*, 250-251.

51. Rousseau, *The Social Contract*, bk. 2, chap. 7.

52. *FL*, 80. See also *ODM*, 223.

53. *RR*, 394. Rousseau expressed this idea in *The Social Contract*, bk. 1, chap. 7.

54. *ODM*, 223.
55. Rousseau, *Discours sur l'origine et les fondements de l'inégalité parmi les hommes*, in *Oeuvres complètes*, 3:133.
56. Ibid., 132.
57. "A Note on Dialectic," *RR*, x.
58. Rousseau, *The Social Contract*, bk. 1, intro.
59. *RR*, x.
60. Rousseau, *The Social Contract*, bk. 2, chap. 7. Cf. Michèle Ansart-Dourlen, "L'Utopie politique de Rousseau et le jacobinisme," in *Le Discours utopique*, papers delivered at a colloquium, Cerisy-la-Salle, 23 July-1 Aug. 1975 (Paris: Union générale d'éditions, 1978), 271-279.
61. "Can Communism Be Liberal?" 861.
62. *EC*, 158.
63. Wilhelm E. Mühlmann, *Messianismes révolutionnaires du tiers monde*, translated by Jean Baudrillard (Paris: Gallimard, 1968), 301. Originally published as *Chiliasmus und Nativismus* (Berlin: Dietrich Reimer, 1961).
64. Julien Freund, "Bref Essai sur les sciences humaines," *Revue de l'enseignement philosophique*, no. 6 (1960): 55.
65. Myrdal, *Das Politische Element in der nationalökonomischen Doktrinbildung*, 1932, 177; cited in Marcuse, *NE*, 13, 271 n. 18.
66. "Theory and Politics," 140.
67. "La Société de l'opulence en procès," *Le Monde*, 11 May 1968, III.
68. Trousson, *Voyages aux pays de nulle part*, 180.
69. Herbert Marcuse, "Thoughts on the Defense of Gracchus Babeuf," in *The Defense of Gracchus Babeuf*, ed. and trans. John Anthony Scott (Boston: University of Massachussetts Press, 1967), 103.
70. Ibid., 98-99.
71. Ibid., 96, citing Gracchus Babeuf, "La Défense de Gracchus Babeuf devant la Haute Cour du Vendôme."
72. Ibid., 98.
73. "Democracy Has, Hasn't a Future," 31.
74. Ibid., 104.
75. Ibid., 104, and Maurice Cranston, "Herbert Marcuse," in *The New Left*, ed. Maurice Cranston (London: Bodley Head, 1970), 86.
76. Marcuse, "Thoughts on the Defense of Gracchus Babeuf," 98.
77. "Democracy Has, Hasn't a Future," 103.
78. Freund, "Anarchie fürht zu Diktatur," 22.
79. "Democracy Has, Hasn't a Future," 101.
80. Marcuse, "Thoughts on the Defense of Gracchus Babeuf," 104.
81. Marcuse, "Discussion on Industrialization and Capitalism," in *Max Weber and the Sociology Today*, ed. Otto Stammer (Oxford, 1971), 185. First German edition 1964. See also Raymond Aron, *Les étapes de la pensée sociologique* (Paris: Gallimard, 1967), 566ff.

82. "Die Gesellschaft als Kuntswerk," *Neues Forum*, 14, nos. 167-168 (Nov.-Dec. 1967): 866.
83. Friedrich Schiller, *Philosophische Schriften* (Basel, 1946), 79, cited by Frederic Jameson, "Marcuse and Schiller," in *Marxism and Form, Twentieth-Century Dialectical Theories of Literature* (Princeton: Princeton University Press, 1971), 88.
84. *NE*, 117.
85. *EL*, 26.
86. Morton Schoolman, "Marcuse's Aesthetics and the Displacement of Critical Theory," in *Telos*, 3, no. 2: 79. As we now know, Marcuse went on to publish *The Aesthetic Dimension* in 1977.
87. Jameson, "Marcuse and Schiller," 90.
88. Emile Lehouck, *Fourier, aujourd'hui* (Paris: Denoël, 1966), 161.
89. Ruyer, *L'Utopie et les utopies*, 218.
90. Ibid., 222.
91. Lehouck, *Fourier, aujourd'hui*, 164.
92. Ibid., 11.
93. Cited by Trousson, *Voyages aux pays de nulle part*, 190.
94. Jean Lacroix, *Le Désir et les désirs*, (Paris: PUF, 1975), 66. Lacroix's work includes "Fourier et le flux du désir," 66-76, and various references to Marcuse, 95-101. See also a review by Umberto Campagnolo, *Comprendre*, nos. 41-42 (1975-76): 260-262.
95. Jean-Paul Thomas, *Libération instinctuelle libération politique, Contribution fouriériste à Marcuse* (Paris: Le Sycomore, 1980). See also a review by Jean-Michel Besnier, "De Marcuse à Fourier," *Esprit*, no. 52 (Apr. 1981): 139-141.
96. Marcuse, "Sommes-nous déjà des hommes?" 26.
97. *EC*, 187.
98. *EC*, 217.
99. Francis Hearn, "Toward a Critical Theory of Play," *Telos*, 9, no. 4 (Winter 1976-77): 145-160.
100. *FL*, 68.
101. *FL*, 63. See also *EL*, 49.
102. *EL*, 22.
103. Besnier, "De Marcuse à Fourier," 141.
104. Herbert Marcuse, "Liberation from the Affluent Society," in *The Dialectics of Liberation*, ed. David Cooper (Harmondsworth: Penguin Books, 1968), 175-192.
105. Ibid., 177; italics mine.
106. Ibid., 184.
107. Ibid., 177.
108. Ibid., 185.
109. Harry Burrows Acton, *The Illusion of an Epoch (London, 1955)*, 233-236.
110. Marx-Engels, "The German Ideology," in *Collected Works*, 5:47.

111. "Socialist Humanism," in *Socialist Humanism*, ed. Erich Fromm (New York: Doubleday, 1965), 112.
112. Marcuse, "Sommes-nous déjà des hommes?" 25-26.
113. "The Realm of Freedom and the Realm of Necessity, A Reconsideration," *Praxis*, 5, nos. 1-2 (1969): 22.
114. See *New Left Review*, 56 (1969): 27-34
115. Marcuse, as cited by Gérard Bergeron, "Qui est Herbert Marcuse?" *Action pédagogique*, nos. 12-13 (1968): 91-92; italics mine.
116. *EL*, 89.
117. Ibid.
118. *CRR*, 47.
119. E. M., "Cops Clear Kant," *San Francisco Good Times*, 12 Feb. 1971, 18.
120. Ibid.
121. Perroux, *François Perroux interroge Herbert Marcuse*, 100.
122. Mme. N. B., "M. François Perroux introduit Marcuse au Collège de France," 11.
123. *EL*, 89.
124. Henri Arvon, "Bakounine," *Encyclopaedia universalis* (1968), 2:1032. See also id., *Michel Bakounine ou la vie contre la science* (Paris: Seghers, 1966), 50.
125. *SM*, 128.
126. *SM*, 125.
127. *RR*, x.
128. *RR*, xiv.
129. Arthur Mitchell, *The Major Works of Herbert Marcuse, A Critical Commentary* (New York: Simon & Schuster, 1975), 98-100, and Gil Green, *The New Radicalism: Anarchist or Marxist?* (New York: International Publishers, 1971), 112-114.
130. *ODM*, 256.
131. *ODM*, 53.
132. Mikhail Bakunin, "Ecrit contre Marx," in *Socialisme autoritaire ou libertaire*, Mikhail Bakunin and Karl Marx (Paris: Union générale d'éditions, 1975), 2:19.
133. Friedrich Engels, "Préface à 'La Guerre des paysans en Allemagne,' " in *Oeuvres choisis*, Friedrich Engels and Karl Marx (Moscow: Editions du progrès, 1975), 248.
134. "Democracy Has, Hasn't a Future," 104.
135. André Reszler, *L'Esthétique anarchiste* (Paris: PUF, 1973), 29, 29-40.
136. Ibid., 31, citing Mikhail Bakunin, *Confession*.
137. "Morale et politique dans la société d'abondance," *FU*, 86.
138. Olivier Reboul, *Langage et idéologie* (Paris: PUF, 1980), 33, citing N. Mandelstam, *Contre tout espoir*.

139. Jules Monnerot, *Sociologie de la révolution* (Paris: Fayarad, 1969), 9.
140. Jacques Ellul, *De la Révolution aux révoltes*, 323; see also "La Révolution qui ne signifie rien," 323-328.
141. Raymond Aron, *La Révolution introuvable.*
142. François Châtelet, Gilles Lapouge, and Olivier Revault d'Allonnes, *La Révolution sans modèle* (Paris-La Haye: Mouton, 1974), 35.
143. Ibid., 131.
144. "Theory and Politics," 150-152.
145. Marcuse, "Protosocialism and Late Capitalism," 36-37.
146. Ibid., 25-26; italics mine.
147. Donald C. Lee, "The Concept of 'Necessity': Marx and Marcuse," *Southwestern Journal of Philosophy*, 6 (Winter 1975): 47-53.
148. Maximilen Rubel, "Utopie et révolution," in *Marx critique du marxisme* (Paris: Payot, 1974), 298. Cf., "Utopia and Revolution," in *Socialist Humanism, An International Symposium*, 2d ed., ed. Erich Fromm (New York: Doubleday, 1966), 211-219. The sentence quoted does not appear in the English version.
149. "Ethics and Revolution," in *Ethics and Society: Original Essays on Contemporary Moral Problems*, ed. Richard T. De George (New York: Doubleday, 1966), 133-147.
150. "Theory and Politics," 126.
151. "The Foundation of Historical Materialism," *SCP*, 29.
152. J. P. Guinle, review of *RR* in *Archives de philosophie du droit*, 15 (1970): 446.
153. "The Obsolescence of Marxism," in *Marx and the Western World*, ed. Nicholas Lobkowicz (Notre Dame, Ind.: University of Notre Dame Press, 1967), 413. Marcuse complained about the omission of the question mark in this title.
154. "Liberation from the Affluent Society," 177ff.
155. "Ethics and Revolution," 134-135.
156. "Réexamen du concept de révolution," *Diogène*, no. 64 (Oct.-Dec. 1968): 23. Cf., "Reexamination of the Concept of Revolution," in *Marx and Contemporary Scientific Thought/Marx et la pensée scientifique contemporaine*, papers presented at a UNESCO symposium on "The Role of Karl Marx in the Development of Contemporary Scientific Theory," 8-10 May 1968 (Paris-La Haye: Mouton, 1968), 476-482.
157. Antony Mark Ruprecht, "Marx and Marcuse: a Comparative Analysis of their Revolutionary Theories," *Dialogue, Journal of Phi Sigma Tau*, 17, nos. 2-3 (April 1975): 51-56.
158. Marx-Engels, "The German Ideology," 5:52-53.
159. Karl Marx, 1859 preface to "A Contribution to the Critique of Political Economy," in *The Marx-Engels Reader*," Robert C. Tucker, ed. (New York: W. W. Norton & Co. Inc., 1972), 5.

160. *RR*, 318, and Herbert Marcuse, "Socialism in the Developed Countries," *International Socialist Journal*, 2, no. 8 (1965): 139-152; cf., 139.
161. Marx, 1859 preface, 5; Marx-Engels, "The German Ideology," 5:54.
162. Marx-Engels, "The Holy Family," in *Collected Works*, 4:36-37.
163. *EL*, 16, 53; *FL*, 98.
164. "Théorie et pratique," in *AC*, 88. This essay originally appeared as "Theorie und Praxis," in *Zeit-Messungen* (Frankfurt am Main: Suhrkamp Verlag, 1975), 21-36.
165. Marx-Engels, "The Holy Family," 4:36-37.
166. Julien Freund, *L'Essence du politique* (Paris: Sireys, 1965), 576-577.
167. *ODM*, 189.
168. "The Reification of the Proletariat," *Canadian Journal of Political and Social Theory*, 3, no. 1 (Winter 1979): 20-23.

Empirical studies bear out the Marcusian theory of the reification of the proletariat, for example: Bennett Berger, *The Working-Class Suburb* (Berkeley: University of California Press, 1960); William Gomberg and Arthur Shostak, eds., *Blue-Collar World* (Englewood Cliffs: Prentice-Hall Inc., 1964); Frederick C. Klein, "Rising Pay Lifts More Blue-Collar Men into a New Affluent Class," *Wall Street Journal*, 5 Apr. 1965, 1 and 12; Daniel Seligman, "The New Masses," in *America as a Mass Society*, ed. Philip Olsen (New York: Free Press, 1963), 244-256.

There is at least one exception, however. John C. Leggett, for example, disagrees with the theory that the workers lack revolutionary potential; see Leggett, *Class, Race and Labor: Working Class Consciousness in Detroit* (Fairlawn: Oxford University Press, 1968).
169. Cf., *RR*, 279.
170. Richard King, "Herbert Marcuse," in *The Party of Eros, Radical Social Thought and the Realm of Freedom* (Chapel Hill: University of North Carolina Press, 1972), 126.
171. Marcuse, "Protosocialism and Late Capitalism," 38. On cultural revolution, see 33-34.
172. Jean-Paul Sartre, "Les Bastilles de Raymond Aron," discussion reported by Serge Lafaurie, *Le Nouvel Observateur*, no. 188 (19-25 June 1968): 27.
173. *EL*, 79; italics mine.
174. Herbert Marcuse, "Varieties of Humanism," *Center Magazine*, 1 (July 1968): 14.
175. Id., "Revolutionary Subject and Self-Government," *Praxis* 5, nos. 1-2 (1969): 326.
176. Ibid., 326.
177. Ibid., 327.
178. "The Obsolescence of Marxism," 409-417.

179. Ibid., 416.
180. Ibid., 417.
181. "Socialism in the Developed Countries," 151.
182. Marx-Engels, "German Ideology," 5:53.
183. *RR*, 319.
184. On the idea of revolution and justification, see Keith Campbell, "Marcuse on the Justification of Revolution," *Politics* (Australasia), 4, no. 2 (Nov. 1969): 161-167; Kai Nielsen, "On the Choice Between Reform and Revolution," *Inquiry*, 14, no. 3 (Autumn 1971), 271-295, reprinted in Virginia Held, Kai Nielsen and Charles Parsons, *Philosophy and Political Action* (New York: Oxford University Press, 1972), 17-51. Julien Freund, "Aspects polémologiques de la violence," *Actions et recherches sociales,* 2-3 (Sept. 1981): 36-51, and "L'Exemple de Marcuse," 40-42.
185. "Réexamen du concept de révolution," 31.
186. *FL*, 90.
187. Louis Wiznitzer "Interview exclusive d'Herbert Marcuse, théoricien révolutionnaire fort doux," *La Presse*, 4 Jan. 1969, 7. This article appeared under the title "Marcuse, le Lénine de la Nouvelle Gauche," in *L'Amérique en crise* (Montreal: Les Editions La Presse, 1972), 357-366; cf., 362.
188. "Ethics and Revolution," 146-147.
189. "Democracy Has, Hasn't a Future," 104.
190. "Cops Clear Kant," 18.
191. *FL*, 81, and *HU*, 10 (preface to the French edition of *ODM*).
192. *FU*, 101.
193. *EC*, 159, cited by Jameson, *Marxism and Form,* 111.
194. "Théorie et pratique," *AC*, 75-76.
195. Höhn and Raulet, "L'Ecole de Francfort en France," *Esprit,* 141.
196. Ibid., 142.
197. Jay, "The Dialectical Imagination," 42-43.
198. Walter Laqueur, *Weimar, Une Histoire culturelle de l'Allemagne des années 20* (Paris: Laffont, [1974] 1978).
199. Alfred Kantorowicz, "La Fin de l'Utopie," *Etudes* (Brussels), no. 4 (1963): 2.
200. Rosa Luxemburg, *Sozialreform oder Revolution* (Leipzig, 1899), cf., *Social Reform or Revolution* (New York, 1937).
201. Ibid., preface.
202. *FL*, 102.
203. Luxemburg, *Sozialreform*, preface.
204. The debate on "socialism or barbarism," the origin of which I have attempted to trace, should not be confused with the name of the journal founded in 1949 by a group of former Trotskyists led by Claude Lefort and Paul Cardan, which ceased publication in 1965, as described in *The Unknown Dimension, European Marxism Since Lenin*, eds. Dick

Howard and Karl E. Klare (New York and London: Basic Books, 1972), 66, 71. Neither should it be confused with the title given by Cornelius Castoriadis, a member of this group, to his six-volume work which appeared in the 10/18 series in France (nos. 751, 806, 825, 857, 1303, and 1304).
205. "The Failure of the New Left," *New German Critique*, 6, no. 3 (Fall 1979): 11.
206. "Réexamen du concept de révolution," 31.
207. "La Liberté et les impératifs de l'Histoire," in K. M'Baye et al., *La Liberté et l'ordre social* (Neuchâtel: Editions de la Baconnière, 1969), 135. This paper and the subsequent discussion were first published in French, although the paper was originally given in English. The discussion was not included in the English version subsequently published as "Freedom and the Historical Imperative," in *Studies in Critical Philosophy* (Boston: Beacon, 1973), 211-223, cf., 216.
208. Michael Loewy, "La Signification méthodologique du mot d'ordre 'socialisme ou barbarie,' " in *Dialectique et révolution, Essais de sociologie et d'histoire du marxisme* (Paris: Anthropos, 1973), 113-129.
209. Ibid., 113, citing G. Lukács, *Histoire et conscience de classe* (Paris: Editions de minuit), 61.
210. Rosa Luxemburg, "The Crisis in German Social Democracy (The Junius Pamphlet: Part One)," in *Selected Political Writings of Rosa Luxemburg*, ed. Dick Howard (New York and London: Monthly Review Press, 1971), 334.
211. "The productive forces created by the modern capitalist mode of production and also the system of distribution of goods established by it have come into burning contradiction with that mode of production itself, and in fact to such a degree that, if the whole of modern society is not to perish, a revolution of the mode of production and distribution must take place." Friedrich Engels, *Herr Eugen Dühring's Revolution in Science (Anti-Dühring)* (New York: International Publishers, [1939] 1966), 174. It is in this passage that the idea of socialism as an alternative choice in a major historical dilemma first appeared.
212. Loewy, *Dialectique et révolution*" 120.
213. "The Failure of the New Left," 11.
214. "Theory et pratique," *AC*, 88-89.
215. Edward Shils, "*Ideology and Utopia* by Karl Mannheim," *Daedalus*, 103, no. 1 (Winter 1973): 83-89.
216. Palmier, *Herbert Marcuse et la Nouvelle Gauche*, 397.
217. Raymond Ruyer, *Les Nuisances idéologiques* (Paris: Calmann-Lévy, 1972), 298.
218. Id., *L'Utopie et les utopies*, 54.
219. Joseph Gabel, "Mannheim et le marxisme hongrois," in *Idéologies* (Paris: Anthropos, 1974), 278. This essay also appeared in *L'Homme et la société*, no. 11 (Jan.-Feb.-Mar. 1969): 127-145. On Mannheim and

Marxism, see also id., "La Crise du marxisme et la psychologie," *Arguments*, 4, no. 18 (1960).

220. "Débats Goldmann-Marcuse (1962)," in *Goldmann*, Sami Nair and Michael Loewy (Paris: Seghers, 1973), 154. On Goldmann-Marcuse, see Lucien Goldmann, "La Pensée de Herbert Marcuse," *La Nef*, no. 36 (1969): 35-57; "A Reply to Lucien Goldmann," *Partisan Review*, 38, no. 4 (1971-1972): 397-400; "Some General Remarks on Lucien Goldmann," *Revue de l'Institut de sociologie de l'Université libre de Bruxelles*, 3-4 (1973): 543-544.

221. Joseph Gabel, "L'Intelligentsia sans attaches (1965)," in *Idéologies*, 294.

222. Ibid., 300.

223. "Débats Goldmann-Marcuse," 154.

224. *ODM*, 189.

225. Karl Mannheim, *Ideology and Utopia, An Introduction to the Sociology of Knowledge*, translated by Louis Wirth and Edward Shils (New York: Harcourt, Brace and World, Inc., 1936), 250.

226. Gérard Raulet, "Encerclement technocratique et dépassement pratique, L'Utopie concrète comme théorie critique," in *Utopie-Marxisme selon Ernst Bloch, Un système de l'inconstructible, Hommages à Ernst Bloch pour son 90e anniversaire publiés sous la direction de Gérard Raulet* (Paris: Payot, 1976), 291-308, cf., 307 n. 49.

227. Armand Cuvillier, "Avant-propos," in Karl Mannheim, *Idéologie et utopie* (Paris: Marcel Rivière, 1956), 7.

228. Jay, *The Dialectical Imagination*, 63.

229. Paul Breines, "Praxis and its Theorists: The Impact of Lukács and Korsch in the 1920's," *Telos*, no. 11 (Spring 1972): 67-103, cf., 95.

230. "Zur Wahrheitsproblematik der soziologischen Methode," in *Die Gesellschaft, Internationale Revue für Sozialismus und Politik*, 6, part 2 (1929): 356-369.

231. Martin Jay, "The Frankfurt School's Critique of Karl Mannheim and the Sociology of Knowledge, *Telos*, 7, no. 2 (Summer 1974): 79. Jay explained that the other members of the school moved away from Mannheim as time went on.

232. Jay, *The Dialectical Imagination*, 63.

233. Karl Mannheim, *Ideologie und Utopie*, 3d ed. (Frankfurt, 1965), 53. "This crucial sentence is missing in all translations," according to Joseph Gabel, "Conscience utopique et fausse conscience," in *Le Discours utopique*, papers delivered at a colloquium, Cerisy-la-Salle, 23 July-1 Aug. 1975 (Paris: Union générale d'éditions, 1978), 37, 46 n. 6.

234. *NE*, 147-148.

235. Cf., Gabel, "Conscience utopique et fausse conscience," 44.

236. James Schmidt, "Critical Theory and the Sociology of Knowledge, A Response to Martin Jay," *Telos*, 7, no. 3 (Fall 1974): 171.

237. Roger Bastide, "Mythes et utopies," *Cahiers internationaux de sociologie*, 28 (Jan.-June 1960): 4. Bastide also quotes Auguste Comte in a similar vein: "Utopias are to the social art what geometric or mechanical models are to their corresponding arts. Such models are accepted as an indispensable step in the most modest constructions, and must therefore be equally necessary in the most elaborate. Furthermore, despite the empirical nature of the political art, all major change in this field has been preceded, one or two centuries earlier, by an analagous utopia that has inspired Humanity's aesthetic spirit with a sixth sense regarding its situation and its needs." *Discours sur l'ensemble du positivisme*, (Editions du Cinquantenaire), 302.
238. Mannheim, *Ideology and Utopia*, 253.
239. For a more detailed comparison between Mannheim and Marcuse, see Joseph L. Devitis, "Mannheim and Marcuse: Social Control in Reconstruction and Revolution," *Southwestern Journal of Philosophy*, 6 (Summer 1975): 129-141. A further comparison between ideology and utopia by Pareto can be found in Julien Freund, *Pareto* (Paris: Seghers), 173.
240. David Kettler, "The Vocation of Radical Intellectuals," *Politics and Society*, 1, no. 1 (Nov. 1970): 34.

Chapter III

1. Jean Marabini, "La Révolution du XXIe siècle sera poétique," Marcuse's last interview, *Les Nouvelles littéraires*, 2-9 Aug. 1979, 3, col. 4-5.
2. Ibid., cols. 1 and 5.
3. *Schriften l: Der deutsche Künstlerroman, Frühe Aufsätze* (Frankfurt: Suhrkamp Verlag, 1978). See commentary by Barry M. Katz, "New Sources of Marcuse's Aesthetics," *New German Critique*, 6, no. 2 (Spring 1979), 176-188.
4. Ben Agger, "The Aesthetic Politics of Herbert Marcuse," *The Canadian Forum*, 53 (Oct. 1973): 24.
5. *ODM*, 63.
6. Agger, "The Aesthetic Politics of Herbert Marcuse," 26, 30.
7. Ben Agger, "The Growing Relevance of Marcuse's Dialectic of Individual and Class," *Dialectical Anthropology*, 4, no. 2 (July 1979): 135.
8. Ibid., 144, 145 n. 14, citing Paul Piccone, "Artificial Negativity," *Telos*, ll, no. 1 (Spring 1978): 43-54.
9. Fred C. Alford, review of *AD*, *Telos*, 14, no. 2 (Summer 1981): 179-188.
10. Marcuse, "Protosocialism and Late Capitalism."
11. Alford, review of *AD*, 188.
12. Ibid., 179, 185.
13. Ibid., 182, citing *AD*, 69.

14. Marcuse, "Protosocialism and Late Capitalism," 28.

15. Alford, review of *AD*, 185. See also p. 181, where he states that Marcuse "can appropriate aspects of Bahro's work to break out of the vicious circle because in *The Aesthetic Dimension* he reconciles himself to the fact that absolute freedom will not be realized in this world."

16. Marcuse, "Protosocialism and Late Capitalism," 32. On the vicious circle, see also ibid., 28ff; *ODM* (1964) 223, 251; "Liberation from the Affluent Society" (1967), 178; *FL* (1970), 36, 80 (this last reference is the only one mentioned by Alford). Rousseau's well-known statement of the problem is given in chap. 2, n. 49).

17. *AD*, 6.

18. L'Express *va plus loin avec ces théoriciens* (Paris: Laffont, 1973), 93.

19. Georges Gusdorf, *Naissance de la conscience romantique au siècle des lumières*, vol. 7 of *Les Sciences humaines et la pensée occidentale* (Paris: Payot, 1976), 443.

20. *EC*, 181ff.

21. Michael Loewy, *Pour une sociologie des intellectuels révolutionnaires; L'Evolution politique de Lukács, 1909-1929* (Paris: Presses universitaires de France, 1976), 28.

22. Paul Breines, "Marxism, Romanticism, and the Case of Georg Lukács: Notes on Some Recent Sources and Situations," *Studies in Romanticism*, no. 16 (Fall 1977): 475-476.

23. Jeffrey Herf, review of Loewy, *Pour une sociologie des intellectuels révolutionnaires*, *Telos*, 11, no. 3 (Fall 1978): 228.

24. Michael Loewy, *Marxisme et romantisme révolutionnaire, Essais sur Lukács et Rosa Luxemburg* (Paris: Le Sycomore, *1979)*.

25. Ibid., 18-19.

26. Ibid., 20.

27. Id., "Marcuse and Benjamin: The Romantic Dimension," *Telos*, 13, no. 2 (Summer 1980): 25-33.

28. Ibid., 26, citing Marcuse, *Der deutsche Künstlerroman*, 43-49, 86, 117-119, 133-143.

29. Katz, "New Sources of Marcuse's Aesthetics," 182, citing Marcuse, *NE*, 229.

30. Jay, "Aesthetic Theory and the Critique of Mass Culture," in *The Dialectical Imagination*, 173-218, see 175.

31. Peter Clecak, "Herbert Marcuse: From History to Myth," in *Radical Paradoxes, Dilemmas of the American Left: 1945-1970* (New York: Harper and Row, 1973), 175-229, see 213.

32. Richard Flacks, "The Importance of the Romantic Myth for the Left," a discussion of Clecak, "Herbert Marcuse: From History to Myth," *Theory and Society*, 2, no. 3, (Fall 1975): 401-414; see 414.

33. Loewy, *Marxisme et romantisme révolutionnaire*, 15, citing Martin Buber, *Utopie et socialisme (Pfade in Utopia)* (Heidelberg: Verlag Lambert

Schneider, 1950), translated by Paul Corset and François Girard (Paris: Aubier-Montaigne, 1977), 89.

34. Eric Volant, *Le Jeu des affranchis, Confrontation Marcuse-Moltmann* (Montreal: Fides, c1976).

35. Ibid., 192.

36. Sam Keen and John Raser, "A Conversation with Herbert Marcuse," *Psychology Today*, 4, no. 9 (1971): 33-36.

37. Brigitte Croisier, "Une Conscience toute neuve," *La Nef*, no. 36 (Jan.-Mar. 1969): 188-189.

38. Michel de Certeau, "Herbert Marcuse, 1898-1979," in *Universalia 1980*, 572-573.

39. Id., "L'Endurance de l'espoir," *Les Nouvelles littéraires*, Aug. 2-9, 1979, 4.

40. Richard Kearney, "Interview with Herbert Marcuse," *The Crane Bag*, 1, no. 1 (Spring 1977): 83-84.

41. H. Peyre, "Romantisme," in *Encyclopaedia Universalis*, 14:367c.

42. Georg Wilhelm Friedrich Hegel, "L'Art romantique," *Esthétique* (Paris: Aubier-Montaigne, 1964), 5:126.

43. Jean-Michel Palmier, "Signification critique du romantisme révolutionnaire," in *Herbert Marcuse et la nouvelle gauche*, 566-571, 582.

44. *ODM*, 60.

45. Michel Haar, *L'Homme unidimensionnel, Marcuse* (Paris: Hatier, 1975), 60-61.

46. *CRR*, 89.

47. *CRR*, 122.

48. Kearney, "Interview with Herbert Marcuse," 81-82.

49. Ibid., 80-81.

50. Herbert Read, "Surrealism and the Romantic Principle," in *Criticism: The Foundations of Modern Literary Judgment*, 96, cited by Gerald Graff, "Aestheticism and Cultural Politics," *Social Research*, 40, no. 2 (Summer 1973), 322.

51. *CRR*, 92.

52. *ODM*, 59.

53. *ODM*, 59.

54. *CRR*, 5.

55. Kearney, "Interview with Herbert Marcuse," 77.

56. Ibid., 80.

57. *CRR*, 86.

58. *AD*, 6.

59. *CRR*, 89.

60. *CRR*, 122.

61. *CRR*, 125.

62. Graff, "Aestheticism and Cultural Politics," 339.

63. Annette T. Rubinstein, review of *AD*, *Science and Society*, 42, no. 4 (1979): 503. The review notes the weakness of Marcuse's argument

against the type of theory put forward by Lukács, since Marcuse makes use of the same concept. Marcuse wrote: "The particular social confrontations are built into the play of metasocial forces between individual and individual, male and female, humanity and nature." *AD*, 27. Lukács, as quoted in the review (p. 504), stated: "The central category and criterion of realistic literature is the type, a particular synthesis which organically binds together the general and the particular in both characters and situations."

64. Kearney, "Interview with Herbert Marcuse," 82. See also *CRR*, 96.

65. "The Relevance of Reality," *Proceedings and Addresses of the American Philosophical Association*, 42 (Oct. 1969): 39-50.

66. Ibid., 50.

67. *Le Monde*, 11 May 1968, 3.

68. "The Relevance of Reality," 50. Marcuse's comments are reminiscent of the opening words of Adorno's *Negative Dialectics*, translated by E. B. Ashton (New York: Seabury Press, 1973), to the effect that philosophy which appears obsolete keeps alive because its moment of realization was missed.

69. Ibid., 47.

70. Karl Marx, "Critique of Hegel's Philosophy of Law, Introduction," *Collected Works*, 3: 187.

71. Preface to *A Contribution to the Critique of Political Economy*, in *The Marx-Engels Reader*, ed. Robert C. Tucker (New York: W. W. Norton & Co., Inc., 1972), 4.

72. Marx-Engels, "The German Ideology," *Collected Works*, 5:37.

73. "Théorie et pratique," *AC*, 75; italics mine. See also *RR*, 319.

74. "The Relevance of Reality," 48; italics mine.

75. *RR*, 322.

76. Jay, *The Dialectical Imagination*, 79.

77. Marx-Engels, "The German Ideology," *Collected Works*, 5:54.

78. *AC*, 75.

79. *AD*, 73.

80. *NE*, 146.

81. *NE*, 154.

82. "The Relevance of Reality," 48-49.

83. *NE*, 119.

84. "A Revolution in Values," in *Political Ideologies*, eds. James A. Gould and Willis H. Truitt (New York: The Macmillan Co., 1973), 331.

85. "The Concept of Negation in the Dialectic," *Telos*, no. 8 (1971): 130-132.

86. *SM*, 111. See also *RR*, 321, and *CRR*, 73-74.

87. Marx, "Economic and Philosophic Manuscripts of 1844," *Collected Works*, 3:277. See also "Marxism and the New Humanity," in *Marxism*

and Radical Religion, Essays toward a Revolutionary Humanism, eds. John C. Raines and Thomas Dean (Philadelphia: Temple University Press, 1970), 8; Arnold Toynbee, "Art as a Form of Reality, in *On the Future of Art* (New York: Viking Press, 1970), 133; *CRR*, 73-74.

88. Cf. George Friedman, "Posing the Problem of Modernity," in *The Political Philosophy of the Frankfurt School*, part II, sect. 10, "The Crisis of the Enlightenment," 11, "The Crisis of Art and Culture," 12, "The Crisis of the Human Psyche," and 13, "The Crisis of History," 109-203.

89. "The Relevance of Reality," 48.

90. "Theory and Politics," 141.

91. *NE*, 131.

92. *CRR*, 121.

93. Theodor Adorno, *Théorie esthétique* (Paris: Klincksieck, 1974). Id., *Aesthetische Theorie, Paralipomena, Frühe Einleitung*, eds. Gretel Adorno and Rolf Tiedemann, vol. 7 of *Complete Works* (1970), 374, as cited by Arato et al., *The Essential Frankfurt School Reader*, 207, 351 n. 77.

94. *EL*, 30ff.

95. *CRR*, 107.

96. Bryan Magee, "Marcuse and the Frankfurt School, Dialogue with Herbert Marcuse," in *Man of Ideas: Some Creators of Contemporary Philosophy*, ed. Bryan Magee (London: British Broadcasting Corporation, 1978), 69-70. See also Habermas's comparison between Marcuse and Benjamin, "Consciousness-raising or Redemptive Criticism—The Contemporaneity of Walter Benjamin," in *New German Critique*, 6, no. 2 (Spring 1979), part I: 32-37.

97. "Art in the One-Dimensional Society," *Arts Magazine*, May 1967, 26-31.

98. Ibid., 26.

99. Jay, "Aesthetic Theory and the Critique of Mass Culture," *The Dialectical Imagination*, 173-218.

100. "The Affirmative Character of Culture," in *NE*, 88-133.

101. "The Struggle Against Liberalism in the Totalitarian View of the State," in *NE*, 3-42.

102. "Base and Superstructure—Reality and Ideology," in *SM*, 105-120.

103. *One-Dimensional Man.*

104. *EL*, and in particular a little-known interview reported in *Les Jeunes et la contestation*, (Paris: Laffont, Bibliothèque Laffont des grands thèmes, no. 93.)

105. *CRR*, passim, and in particular 83-84.

106. Marcuse's ideas on "culture industry" were similar to those of Horkheimer and Adorno in 1944, given a wider audience by Adorno in 1963 and 1967; cf., David Held, *Introduction to Critical Theory* (Berkeley: University of California Press, 1980), pp. 90ff. The notion of

popular culture allows for the idea that a certain element of culture originates spontaneously with the masses, whereas today, according to the members of the Frankfurt School, culture is controlled and manipulated, and its autonomy is threatened by industrial civilization. This is why they finally preferred the expression "culture industry" to "mass culture."

107. "The Struggle Against Liberalism in the Totalitarian View of the State," *NE*, 3-42.

108. Ibid., 42.

109. *SM*, 107.

110. *SM*, 110.

111. *SM*, 115.

112. *SM*, 117; italics mine.

113. *SM*, 116.

114. *SM*, 116.

115. *SM*, 120.

116. *SM*, 118.

117. "Préface à l'edition française," *HU*, 7; cf., *ODM*, xvi.

118. "The Concept of Essence," in *NE*, 65.

119. "De l'ontologie à la technologie; Les Tendances de la société industrielle," *Arguments*, 4, no. 18 (1960): 54-59.

120. "The Language of Total Administration," and "The New Forms of Control" in *ODM*.

121. *SM*, 117.

122. *ODM*, 63.

123. "Préface à l'edition française," *HU*, 10.

124. *ODM*, 248.

125. Cf., Gérard Raulet, "La Révolution impossible? En hommage à Herbert Marcuse," *Allemagnes d'aujourd'hui*, (Sept. 1979):25.

126. *NE*, 119.

127. *AD*, 13.

128. Vincent Geoghegan, *Reason and Eros, The Social Theory of Herbert Marcuse* (London: Pluto Press, 1981), 28.

129. Ernst Bloch, "Le Concept de fonction utopique," in *Le Principe Espérance* (1959; Paris: Gallimard, 1976), 174-216. Pierre Furter, "Utopie et marxisme selon Ernst Bloch," *Archives de sociologies des religions*, no. 21 (Jan.-June 1966): 3-21, see 9-13. Laënnec Hurbon, "Trois fonctions de l'utopie," in *Ernst Bloch, utopie et espérance* (Paris: Cerf, 1974), 73-75.

130. Paul Ricoeur, "The Task of the Political Educator," translated by David Stewart, *Philosophy Today* 17, no.2/4 (Summer 1973): 140-152, see 150-151; "Prévision économique et choix éthique," *Esprit*, (Feb. 1966), reprinted in *Histoire et vérité*, 3d ed. (Paris: Seuil, n.d.) 301-316, see 312-315; 'La Fonction constituante de l'utopie,' in "L'Herméneu-

tique de la sécularisation, Foi, Idéologie, Utopie," in *Herméneutique de la sécularisation*, 49-69, see 59.

131. Pavel Kovaly, "Contemporary Functions of the Marxist Utopia," in *Utopia/Dystopia?*, ed. Peyton E. Richter (Cambridge, Mass.: Schenkman, 1975), 89-92.

132. George Friedman, *The Political Philosophy of the Frankfurt School*, 140-141, 158.

133. François Chirpaz, "Aliénation et utopie," *Esprit*, no. 377 (Jan. 1969): 88; italics mine.

134. Parvis Piran, 'Marcuse's Aesthetic Perpective,' in "Marcuse and the Problem of Instrumental Rationality," *Mid-American Review of Sociology*, 2, no. 2 (Winter 1977): 19-28, see 24-28.

135. Michel Haar, *L'Homme unidimensionnel, Marcuse*, 76.

136. Roger Garaudy, *Perspective de l'homme* (Paris: Presses universitaires de France, 1969), 373-374.

137. "Remarks on a Redefinition of Culture," *Daedalus*, 94, no. 1 (Winter 1965): 207; italics mine.

138. Geoghegan, *Reason and Eros, The Social Theory of Herbert Marcuse*, 28.

139. Furter, "Utopie et marxisme selon Ernst Bloch," 9-13. Hurbon, "Trois Fonctions de l'utopie," 73-75.

140. Ricoeur, "Prévision économique et choix éthique," 314.

141. Ibid., 312; italics mine.

142. Id., "The Task of the Political Educator," 150; italics mine.

143. Id., "Prévision économique et choix éthique," 313.

144. Id., "The Task of the Political Educator," 147.

145. Kovaly, "Contemporary Functions of the Marxist Utopia," 89-92.

146. Adam Schaff, *Marxism and the Human Individual* (New York: McGraw-Hill, 1971), 135, cited by Kovaly, 89.

147. Ricoeur, "The Task of the Political Educator," 145.

148. Id., "L'Herméneutique de la sécularisation, Foi, Idéologie, Utopie," 59.

149. *ODM*, 238-239; see also *AD*, 6.

150. Georg Wilhelm Friedrich Hegel, *Philosophy of Fine Art*, translated by F. P. B. Osmaston (New York, 1975), 1:42-43, 263-264, cited by Friedman, *The Political Philosophy of the Frankfurt School*, 141.

151. Cf., Marcuse, in chap. 2 of *EL*; Max Horkheimer, "Authority in the Family," in *Critical Theory, Selected Essays* (New York: Seabury Press, 1972), 47-128; Benjamin and Adorno, as cited by Friedman, *The Political Philosophy of the Frankfurt School*, 138 n. 6.

152. Walter Benjamin, "The Work of Art in an Age of Mechanical Reproduction," in *Illuminations: Essays and Reflections* ed. Hannah Arendt (New York [1953] 1968), 241-242, as cited by Friedman, *The Political Philosophy of the Frankfurt School*, 148 n. 30.

153. Friedman, 158-159.
154. Ibid., 159.
155. *EC*, 144.
156. Friedman, 159.
157. *ODM*, 249; see also 228-229.
158. "Débats Goldmann-Marcuse," 154.
159. *AD*, 32.
160. *EL*, 24, 19-20.
161. Plato, *The Statesman*, 293b; Karl Popper, *The Open Society and Its Enemies: The Spell of Plato* (Princeton: Princeton University Press, [1962] 1966), 165.
162. Plato, *Republic*, 500e-501a.
163. Ibid., 541a.
164. Id., *The Statesman*, 293d-e.
165. *FU*, 86.
166. Popper, *The Open Society*, 166-168.
167. Sources on Popper-Marcuse relations within the context of these well-known controversies are, in chronological order, as follows: Karl Popper, "Reason or Revolution?" in T. W. Adorno et al., *The Positivist Dispute in German Sociology* (New York: Harper and Row, 1976); *Times Literary Supplement*, "Dialectical Methodology," 12 Mar. 1970; Wolf Lepenies, "Anthropology and Social Criticism: A View on the Controversy between Arnold Gehlen and Jürgen Habermas," *The Human Context*, 3, no. 2 (July 1971): 205-248; H. T. Wilson, "Science, Critique, and Criticism: The Open Society 'Revisited,' " in *On Critical Theory*, ed. John O'Neill (New York: The Seabury Press, 1976), 205-230; Jean-François Malherbe, "La 'Théorie critique' et les limites du rationalisme de Popper," in *La Philosophie de Karl Popper et le positivisme logique* (Paris: Presses universitaires de France, 1976), 229-254; L. J. Ray, "Critical Theory and Positivism: Popper and the Frankfurt School," *Philosophy of Social Sciences*, 9, no. 2, (1979): 149-173.
168. Popper, "Reason or Revolution?" 244.
169. *Theodor W. Adorno zum Gedächtnis* (Frankurt am Main: Suhrkamp Verlag, 1971), 50-51.
170. Magee, "Marcuse and the Frankfurt School," 73.
171. Popper, "Reason or Revolution?" 245.

Chapter IV

1. Martin Jay, "Metapolitics of Utopianism," *Dissent*, 17, no. 4 (July-Aug. 1970): 350. In Marcuse's article on "Art and Revolution" published in 1972, he himself spoke of "metapolitics" (cf., *CRR*, 104).
2. *ODM*, 4.
3. Raymond Aron, *Essai sur les libertés* (Paris: Calmann-Lévy [1965] 1976), 27, citing Alexis de Tocqueville, "Preface," *L'Ancien Régime et la révolution*.

4. Crawford Brough Macpherson, *The Political Theory of Possessive Individualism—Hobbes to Locke* (Oxford: Oxford University Press [1962] 1983). Id., *The Life and Times of Liberal Democracy* (Oxford: Oxford University Press, [1977] 1980).
5. *RT*, 87.
6. *NE*, xix.
7. Freund, *L'Essence du politique*, 650-651.
8. *RR*, "Supplementary Epilogue Written in 1954," 439.
9. *RT*, 88.
10. Roger Garaudy, *Perspectives de l'homme: Existentialisme, pensée catholique, structuralisme, marxisme* (Paris: Presses universitaires de France, 1969), 373-374.
11. Ibid., 375.
12. Ibid.
13. *ODM*, 18.
14. André Gorz, "Techniques, techniciens et lutte des classes," *Temps modernes*, no. 301 (1971): 144.
15. *FL*, 62.
16. *FL*, 64.
17. *ODM*, 4.
18. George Kateb, "The Political Thought of Herbert Marcuse," - *Commentary*, 49, no. 1 (Jan. 1970): 48-49.
19. *RR*, 288.
20. *CRR*, 134.
21. *AC*, 75.
22. *FL*, 64, and *ODM*, 4.
23. "Marcuse Defines His New Left Line," translated by Helen Weaver, in *The American Experience*, eds. Harold Jaffe and John Tytell (New York: Harper and Row, 1970), 126.
24. John Fry, *Marcuse—Dilemma and Liberation. A Critical Analysis* (Stockholm: Almqvist and Wiksell, 1974), 19-20.
25. *ODM*, 34; *NE*, xiv-xv; *EL*, 80.
26. *ODM*, 34. See also *EL*, 84-85.
27. *SM*, 60.
28. *SM*, 83.
29. *NE*, 248; *SM*, 19-20.
30. *EL*, 13-14.
31. *ODM*, xiii, 18; *SM*, 60; *NE*, xv.
32. *NE*, 248; *ODM*, 34, 242.
33. *EL*, viiff.
34. *FL*, 93.
35. *EL*, 80, 82.
36. *FL*, 95.
37. *ODM*, 23.

38. *EL*, 82. It is perhaps worth noting here that, when asked by Marcel Rioux about the role of small national entities such as Quebec, Marcuse considered that they were too small a unit to be significant, and that the independence of Quebec would be a superficial and peripheral change. *Forces*, no. 22 (1973): 60.

39. *ODM*, 49.

40. *ODM*, 189.

41. *ODM*, xvi, 220-221.

42. Julien Freund, "A propos du besoin et de la violence: Les Rapports entre l'économique, le politique et la nature humaine," *Paysans*, 19, no. 110 (Feb.-Mar. 1975): 10, citing: Frédéric Bastiat, *Harmonies économiques*, vol. 6 *Oeuvres complètes* (Paris: Guillaumin, 1893), 589. Claude Henri de Rouvroy, Comte Saint-Simon, *De la réorganisation de la société européenne*, vol. 15 of *Oeuvres de Saint-Simon et Enfantin*, 248. Auguste Comte, *Cours de philosophie positive*, vol. 6, 57th lesson.

43. *ODM*, 119-120, citing Theodor W. Adorno, "Ideologie," in *Ideologie* (Luchterhand: Neuwied, 1961), 262ff.

44. Reboul, *Langage et idéologie*, 13.

45. Ibid., 21.

46. Ibid., 21-25. Julien Freund, *L'Essence du politique*, 412-441, and "Qu'est-ce que la politique idéologique?" *Revue européenne des sciences sociales*, 17, no. 46 (1979): 139-146. Jean Baechler, *Qu'est-ce que l'idéologie?* (Paris: Gallimard, 1976), particularly the chapter on "Les Fonctions de l'idéologie," 63-105.

47. Olivier Reboul, "La Violence et l'idéologie," *Dialogue*, 17, no. 3 (Sept. 1978), 431-441.

48. William Leiss, et al., "Marcuse as Teacher," 425.

49. Cf., Raymond Aron, *Plaidoyer pour une Europe décadente* (Paris: Laffont, 1977), and Julien Freund, *La Fin de la Renaissance* (Paris: Presses universitaires de France).

50. *FU*, 86.

51. Ludwig Feuerbach, *Cours sur l'histoire de la philosophie moderne* (1935), cited by Marcuse in the epigraph to *Philosophie et révolution* (Paris: Denoël-Gonthier, *1969).*

52. Id., *Principes de philosophie* (1843-1844), cited by Marcuse in the epigraph to *Philosophie et révolution.*

53 Loewy, *Marxisme et romantisme révolutionnaire*, 14-15.

54. "The Realm of Freedom and the Realm of Necessity, A Reconsideration," 20.

55. "Art in the One-Dimensional Society," 26.

56. "The Movement in a New Era of Repression," *Berkeley Journal of Sociology*, 16 (1971-72): 9.

57. "The Failure of the New Left," 11.

58. Baechler, *Qu'est-ce que l'idéologie?*, 69.

59. "The Realm of Freedom and the Realm of Necessity, A Reconsideration," 20.
60. "Theory and Politics," 136.
61. *ODM*, 234.
62. Karl R. Popper, "Utopia and Violence," in *Conjectures and Refutations: The Growth of Scientific Knowledge* (New York: Harper, 1968), 358. This article first appeared in *The Hibbert Journal*, 46 (1948).
63. *NE* 143. On the word "Eigensinn," see commentary by Pierre V. Zima, *L'Ecole de Francfort* (Paris: Editions universitaires), 24.
64. *FU*, 86-87.
65. "Democracy Has, Hasn't a Future," 104.
66. Reboul, *Langage et idéologie*, 23.
67. This connection between total ideology and utopia is analyzed by Baechler, *Qu'est-ce que l'idéologie?*, 95, *101, 120, 315*.
68. Giovanni Busino, citing Baechler in a review of *Qu'est-ce que l'idéologie?* in *Revue européenne des sciences sociales*, 17, no. 48 (1979): 51-52.
69. Jean Marabini, "Les Derniers Désirs de Marcuse," *Le Devoir*, 7 Aug. 1979, 4.
70. *FL*, 102.
71. Kearney, "Interview with Herbert Marcuse," 84.
72. "Theory and Politics," 136.
73. *RR*, x.
74. *ODM*, 189.
75. "Le Dialogue de deux penseurs 'contestataires,' " *Paris-Match*, 23 Mar. 1979, 9. Elsewhere Marcuse stated, "I have tried to base my analysis on the facts," in "Répression et liberté," in *La Liberté et l'ordre social*, proceedings of the 22d Rencontres internationales de Genève (Neuchâtel: Editions de la Baconnière, 1969), 273. The latter appeared in English as "Freedom and the Historical Imperative," in *Studies in Critical Philosophy* (Boston: Beacon, 1973).
76. Wolff, "Herbert Marcuse: A Personal Reminiscence," 6.
77. The ideas expressed in this paragraph are based on a consideration of the distinction between genus and species in Aristotle, with reference to: Julien Freund, "Sens et responsabilité de la réflexion philosophique à l'heure actuelle," *Revue de l'enseignement philosophique*, no. 2 (1962): 1-16, cf., 2, 9, 10; Paul Ricoeur, *Le Volontaire et l'involontaire* (Paris: Aubier-Montaigne, 1967), 18.
78. Jean Roy, "Millénarisme et situationnisme," *Philosophiques*, 8, no. 1 (Apr. 1981): 27. See also, id., "La 'Tolérance répressive,' nouvelle ruse de la Raison d'Etat?" 488.
79. Russell Jacoby, "Herbert Marcuse: The Philosopher as Perpetual Scandal," *Los Angeles Times*, 5 Aug. 1979, sec. 5, p. 2, col. 1.
80. "Marcuse Defines His New Left Line," 117.
81. *Time, The Weekly Magazine*, "Professors, One-Dimensional Philosopher," Canadian ed., 22 Mar. 1968, 67.

82. Raymond Aron, *La Révolution introuvable*, 119.
83. Donald Robinson, *The 100 Most Important People in the World Today* (New York: Putnam, 1970), 275.
84. *AC*, 88.
85. *AC*, 75.
86. Mikel Dufrenne, *Subversion-perversion* (Paris: Presses universitaires de France, 1977).
87. Ibid., 147.
88. Ibid., 153.
89. Ibid., 146, 151-152, 171. On "utopian action," see also id., *Art et politique* (Paris: Union générale d'éditions, 1974), 275-315.
90. *FL*, 68.
91. *FL*, 92.
92. "Marcuse Defines His New Left Line," 135.
93. "Theory and Politics," 136. On the politics of provocation, see *EL*, 64.

Chapter V

1. Jean Jacques Rousseau, *Emile*, cited by Gérard Raulet, "Eschatologie et utopie ou la découverte de l'histoire," in *Stratégies de l'utopie*, Pierre Furter, Gérard Raulet, et al. (Paris: Galilée, 1979), 179 n. 2.
2. *RR* (1954 ed.), x.
3. *NE*, 182.
4. *FL*, 101.
5. *FL*, 96.
6. *SM*, 180.
7. *SM*, 183-185.
8. "Sommes-nous déjà des hommes?" 21-27.
9. Max Weber, "Le Métier et la vocation d'homme politique," in *Le Savant et le politique* (Paris: Plon, 1959), 99-185. See also "Politics as a Vocation," in *From Max Weber*, eds. H. H. Gerth and C. Wright Mills (New York: 1946).
10. Ricoeur, "The Tasks of the Political Educator," 142-152.
11. *FL*, 43.
12. Ibid.
13. Ricoeur, "The Tasks of the Political Educator," 150.
14. Ibid., 149-50.
15. Ibid., 151.
16. "Conclusion," in *Max Weber and the Sociology Today*, ed. "Otto Stammer (Oxford, 1971), 185.
17. Weber, "Le Métier et la vocation d'homme politique," 174.
18. "Freedom and the Historical Imperative," 216.
19. "When Law and Morality Stand in the Way," *Society*, 10, no. 6 (Sept.-Oct. 1973), 23.

20. "Marcuse Defines His New Left Line" 127.
21. *FL*, 90.
22. *RT*, 103. See also Pierre Mertens, "Violence 'institutionnelle,' violence 'démocratique' et régression," *La Violence et ses causes*, (UNESCO, 1980), 227-248.
23. *RT*, 99.
24. *RT*, 122.
25. *RT*, 106.
26. "Theory and Politics," 136.
27. *RT*, 109.
28. *RT*, 81.
29. *FL*, 64.
30. *ODM*, 4.
31. *FL*, 62.
32. *ODM*, xiii.
33. "Ethics and Revolution," 133.
34. Ibid., 135.
35. Ibid., 133.
36. On the origin of the modern concept of the unjust enemy in Kant's philosophy, see C. Schmitt, *Der Nomos der Erde* (Cologne, 1950), chap. 3, para. 2, 141ff., as cited by Freund, *L'Essence du politique*, 614-615. Regarding war, Kant wrote that neither of the two parties can therefore be described as an unjust enemy (which already presumes a judgment), but that it is the *issue* which decides which side is right (*Projet de Paix perpétuelle*, sect. 1, para. 2). He also defined the unjust enemy as he whose publicly expressed wish (either in word or deed) reveals a maxim which, if set forth as a general rule, would make peace between peoples impossible, whereas the state of nature ought, on the contrary, to be considered eternal. Kant defined the just enemy as one whom it would be unjust on his part to resist, although in that case it would no longer be an enemy. *Métaphysique des moeurs, Doctrine du droit*, part 2, "Le Droit public," par. 60. See also Julien Freund, 'Morale et violence, L'Exemple de Marcuse,' in "Aspects polémologiques de la violence," *Actions et recherches sociales*, nos. 1-2 (Sept. 1981): 40-42.
37. Weber, *Le Savant et le politique*, 180-181.
38. *NE*, 119.
39. *CRR*, 130.
40. *EL*, 28.
41. Immanuel Kant, "Of Beauty as the Symbol of Morality," in *Critique of Judgment*, trans. J. H. Bernard (London: Macmillan, 1892), para. 59.
42. *EC*, 174; *CRR*, 73-74; see also *CRR*, 66-67, and *EL*, 28, 32.
43. Max Weber, "Essai sur le sens de la 'neutralité axiologique' dans les sciences sociologiques et économiques," in *Essais sur la théorie de la science*, trans. Julien Freund (1917; Paris: Plon, 1965), 425, 428.

44. *EL*, 26.
45. *EL*, 28.
46. *FL*, 65.
47. *EL*, 24; *FL*, 68.
48. *EC*, 228.
49. *CRR*, 74.
50. *EL*, 24.
51. *EL*, 48.
52. *EL*, 49, 21; *FL*, 63.
53. "Theory and Politics," 147.
54. "Political Preface, 1966," *EC*, xxvii.
55. "Liberation from the Affluent Society," 190-191. On the idea of political philosophy as therapy, see Gertrude A. Steuernagel, *Political Philosophy as Therapy: Marcuse Reconsidered* (Westport, Conn.: Greenwood Press, 1979).
56. *FL*, 86; *RT*, 112.
57. *ODM*, 158.
58. *ODM*, 235.
59. *ODM*, 227.
60. *ODM*, 154, 235.
61. *ODM*, 156-158, 166.
62. *FL*, 96.
63. *AD*, 36.
64. Marabini, "La Révolution du XXIe siècle sera poétique," 3.

Conclusion

1. Reinhard Lettau, "Herbert Marcuse and the Vulgarity of Death," *New German Critique*, 6, no. 3 (Fall 1979): 20.
2. *AD*, 59.
3. *AD*, 60.

Index